THIS MINISTRY AND SERVICE

THIS MINISTRY
AND SERVICE

A Textbook of Pastoral Care
and Parish Administration

by The Very Rev. FRANK D. GIFFORD, PH.D., S.T.D.

Dean of the Divinity School in Philadelphia

Morehouse-Gorham Co. NEW YORK

PRINTED IN THE UNITED STATES OF AMERICA

To the students of the Divinity School
in Philadelphia
whom I have been privileged to teach
as
Professor of Pastoral Theology

Foreword

This book is written because of suggestions from many persons that it would be helpful to have a textbook in Pastoral Theology and Parish Administration, written by one who has served many years in the parish ministry, and also as dean and professor in a theological school. It contains the experience of many in the active work of the Church, with ideas and suggestions from scores of faithful men of God, too numerous to mention.

Yet, after all, the responsibility for what is here said must be borne solely by the author. He is conscious that some will disagree with ideas and suggestions herein expressed, but it is his fervent hope and prayer that this book will prove helpful to young men who are going out as champions of the faith in these difficult times. It is his conviction that the Christian ministry is the most difficult, adventurous, inspiring, and truly rewarding of all vocations.

FRANK D. GIFFORD.

Contents

THIS MINISTRY AND SERVICE

The Pastoral Task Today

Jesus saith unto him, Feed my sheep.

—St. John 21:17.

Shepherds. Jesus spoke of Himself as the Good Shepherd who knew His sheep and gave His life for them. Though crowds followed Him and heard His words gladly, still His great concern was the needs of individuals. He has been called the greatest personal worker of all time. He commissioned the Apostles to feed His sheep, to be shepherds of the flock. Throughout all the centuries of Christian history men have been called to be pastors, to minister to those entrusted to their care, but the pastoral task has varied greatly with changing conditions. St. Paul was concerned with the problems of the Gentile converts in Corinth and the moral degeneracy of that pagan city. He wrote to those in Galatia, urging that they stand fast in their Christian liberty and be not bewitched into bondage to the legalism of the law. St. Timothy and St. Titus were given practical advice concerning pastoral work with the congregations in Ephesus and Crete.

History. In later centuries we find great leaders like St. Ambrose in Milan and St. Augustine in Africa, inspiring their clergy to instruct and guide their people in relation to the Roman government and the heresies of their times. The pastoral task in times of invasion and persecution was quite different from that in the days of peace and prosperity. The village priest of the Middle Ages was often the only learned and educated person in his community. In those days in England or France practically everybody would be baptized and belong to the local church. It was common for a man to be born, married, and buried in the same village. Even the Reformation did not change some things, for whole communities and nations became Protestant or remained under the Papal authority, so that the local pastor or priest retained his leadership and authority.

The Present Situation. Very different conditions are found in the twentieth century in the United States. He who would preach the Gospel and administer the sacraments in these days is confronted with situations and problems of which the minister of bygone centuries never dreamed. The old authority of being the parish priest of the whole community has vanished. Now, even in small villages, there are many competing religious bodies. There is the Roman Catholic Church, strong in numbers and in the discipline of obedience to authority. There are the larger Protestant Churches: Methodist,

Baptist, Lutheran, Presbyterian, which seem, to the average American, to teach and preach essentially the same Gospel in slightly different ways. There is the Anglican Communion throughout the world, known in the United States as the Protestant Episcopal Church, claiming to be both Protestant and Catholic, with some parishes stressing the evangelical Gospel and others the administration of the sacraments. There are also many sects, such as Jehovah's Witnesses, Pillar of Fire, Assemblies of God, Father Divine's Heavens and Angels, each claiming to have the true Christian message. To add to the religious confusion, there are also such unusual religious bodies as the Church of the Latter-Day Saints with a Temple and Tabernacle in Salt Lake City and the Christian Science Church with the Mother Church in Boston.

Changing Conditions. Conditions of living—social, political, economic—are also vastly different from the world of bygone pastoral life. The modern pastor, for example, ministers to a changing procession, rather than to a stabilized community. Mid-twentieth-century Americans have extreme mobility of residence. Instead of families being established in one parish for generations, in many places a person who has stayed five years is an old-timer, and to live for a decade in one place makes a man almost a founding father. One rector called on a couple who had moved twenty-seven times in thirteen years, who said they had never stayed in one place long enough to have their children baptized. Christian pastors today must deal with the restlessness and transiency of American life.

Variety.   Furthermore, a young man who prepares for the ministry and service of the Church today must realize the immense variety of pastoral life and work. He may become vicar of two or three country churches, many miles distant from each other. He may become curate in an endowed downtown church in the business district of a great metropolis. The parishioners will come from a distance on Sundays, for few live near the church. Such a parish may develop a strong weekday ministry for those who work in stores and offices. Another young man may be fortunate in serving the growing suburban church, with scores of new families moving in, an overflowing Church School, and the necessity of a building campaign for a new parish house. Still another may face the peculiar circumstances in a college community with thousands of students, or a summer or winter resort city, such as Atlantic City or Miami. Perhaps his pews will be crowded with visitors at certain times and almost deserted at other seasons.

Interpretation.   The Christian pastor in America today is expected to understand the conditions under which his people live and work, so that he may interpret the Gospel to them in terms they will comprehend. He may deal almost exclusively with commuting business executives, who catch the 8:18 every morning to go to the city. He may serve among the dingy houses and apartments of an industrial city, where the noise and smoke of factories and the activities of labor unions dominate the lives of his people. Perhaps he will be in a cultured community, and discover learned professors sitting in his pews and inquiring students challenging him with difficult questions. Possibly his church will be near an army post or a naval station. Then there will be throngs of young men far from their homes, and families of soldiers and sailors who live in furnished rooms.

The Unchanging Gospel. Yet the modern pastor will discover that the Gospel he preaches and the task he performs are essentially the same as in all generations, despite the wide variety of living conditions. Jesus Christ is the same, yesterday, today, and forever. Human needs and problems may seem different on the surface, but temptations and sins are basically the same in all centuries. The wheat farmer in Kansas and the stockbroker in Wall Street are both human beings, with the same temptations to worship false gods and the same need for saving grace. The man on the assembly line in Detroit and the sharecropper in the cotton fields of Mississippi both need to know themselves as children of God, inheritors of the Kingdom of Heaven, rather than as mere pawns in a futile game or cogs in an industrial machine.

Administration. Parish methods may vary greatly from the large city parish to the struggling country mission, but both may face a diminishing population in their neighborhoods and the necessity of changing old ways to meet new conditions. Preaching may be a different thing for the big-city rector with his radio broadcasts, but even the rural pastor can now use the latest audio-visual methods, and the whole country is covered with radio stations and television channels. Personal, man-to-man work, however, will never be out of date. It is significant that more and more emphasis is being laid upon pastoral counseling and the need for casework in clinical pastoral training. In all our study of group methods and parish ways and means, let us never forget that the good shepherd of souls must know his sheep personally and lay down his life in service for them.

+ 2 +

Holy Baptism

Do sign him with the sign of the Cross.

—Book of Common Prayer, p. 280.

History. From the earliest times Baptism has been regarded in the Christian Church as a sacrament commanded by Christ and necessary for all who would be in the way of salvation. Jesus had said to Nicodemus, "Except a man be born of water and of the Spirit, he cannot enter into the kingdom of God." On the first Pentecost St. Peter said to the inquirers, "Repent, and be baptized every one of you." The little groups of early Christians thought of themselves as living in the outward, material world, but belonging to the spiritual realm, the Kingdom of Heaven. Each local fellowship was a little colony of Heaven. Baptism was the appointed means whereby one became a citizen of this spiritual country. In the outward world they were subject to Caesar, surrounded by evil influences; but in the Christian fellowship they were in the realm of grace, set free from the power of sin, incorporated into the Body of Christ.

19

Infant Baptism.   It was natural for whole families
and households to come by Baptism into this fellowship. The Master had taken little ones into His arms
and blessed them, saying, "for of such is the Kingdom
of God." From the Apostolic days, infants were baptized and regarded as members of the Church just as
much as adults. Only much later in history did the
idea arise that one must be old enough and good
enough to "join the Church." Parents believed it was
their duty to pledge the child to the highest and best
in life, giving him spiritual training and Christian nurture. The great majority of Christians in all centuries
have believed in infant Baptism, desiring their little
ones to know God as the heavenly Father and themselves as real members of the fellowship of His Church.
No wise parent would permit a child to grow up without national citizenship and secular education, for this
would handicap him for life. Likewise, little children
have the right to receive the best while young, to grow
up as members of the Church, to be fully equipped to
face the battles of life.

Godparents.   Children who are too young to speak
for themselves must always act through their parents.
Fathers and mothers decide questions and act in ways
that affect the whole course of life. Only when a child
comes to years of discretion and maturity is he able to
speak and act for himself. Hence the Church has al-

ways had godparents or sponsors, chosen by the parents. When possible, there should be two men and one woman for a boy, two women and one man for a girl. Godparents should be baptized persons, in hearty sympathy with the service of Holy Baptism, ready to pledge in the child's name that he will renounce evil, believe Christian truth, and do God's will and commandments. It is the privilege of the sponsors to give the child his Christian name at Baptism and to take an active, loving interest in the Christian nurture of the child ever after. Godparents also pledge themselves to see that the child, when sufficiently instructed, be brought to the Bishop for Confirmation. It is obvious that they should not be persons opposed to Confirmation, but rather that they themselves be confirmed persons. It is a mistake for parents, misunderstanding the meaning of Holy Baptism, to ask Baptists or Roman Catholics to act as godparents, since they cannot honestly make promises contrary to their own principles.

Preparation. The pastor should require sufficient notice in advance, so that he can have interviews with the parents and give instruction to them, and, if possible, to the godparents. This is pastoral work of the highest importance. Frequently it will be advisable for the minister to give a brief preface to the Baptismal Office, addressing the sponsors concerning their part in the service and reminding them of the sacred obligations they are about to take. Certificates are now available to give to godparents with definite instructions for them. Also, before the service all necessary facts concerning the child should be obtained, using blanks printed for this purpose. Baptismal certificates ought to be given to the parents without delay and entries should be made in the parish register. In many parishes a card index is kept for all birthdays and anniversaries, so that records are available for the Font Roll.

Adult Baptism. Among early Christians a long period of instruction preceded the Baptism of adults. This is true today in foreign mission lands and should be true in all cases where the person has little knowledge of the Christian faith and life. Instruction might well be based upon the baptismal vows, including the renunciation of evil, the Creed as a statement of the faith, the Ten Commandments, and the Summary of the Law. The adult who seeks to be baptized must speak for himself in renouncing sin, professing the Christian faith, and pledging loyalty to Christ and the Church. There should be a penitential preparation with confession of sin, but no absolution pronounced since in Holy Baptism this grace is fully given. In the Church, from early times, confession with absolution by the priest has been for post-baptismal sins. No sponsors are required for adult Baptism, but two or more witnesses should be present and their names recorded. They represent the whole Church in expressing a hearty welcome into the fellowship of Christ.

The Font.   This is usually placed near the door of the church to signify that Baptism is the sacrament of entrance into the Church. It should be spotlessly clean and not used for floral decorations or any purpose other than Baptism. Clean water, warmed a little in cold weather, should be placed in the font before the service. Many parishes use a silver or brass basin inside the font. Afterwards the water is poured out upon the ground. A white stole, or one with purple on one side and white on the other, should be placed at the font. When two colors are used, the purple is worn until the Sursum Corda, and then the white. Purple signifies penitence, while white is the color of purity and joy.

Methods.   A small child should be held firmly on the left arm of the minister, leaving the right free to pour water three times upon the child's head, which is held over the font. Older children and adults may stand holding their heads over the font. The thumb is used in blessing the water, in the prayer before naming the child, and also in making the sign of the Cross upon the forehead. It is an ancient custom that males should be baptized first and that younger children have precedence. Because of obvious difficulties, the priest should memorize important parts of the service and not depend upon the book.

Time and Place. Since Baptism is the sacrament of initiation into the fellowship of the Church, it should not be a private matter with only the family and a few friends present. In the English Prayer Book there is a rubric that Baptism ought to be "when the most number of people are gathered together." In the American Prayer Book the time suggested is "after the Second Lesson at Morning or Evening Prayer." Because this would prolong the service unduly in large parishes, the custom is growing of having the service in the afternoon once a month. Then the whole parish is urged to come to welcome the new members and to join the rector in saying, "We receive this child into the congregation of Christ's flock." When the group or district system is used, all persons living in a certain area are invited, when a child from that neighborhood is to be baptized. In some instances, unofficial godparents are appointed in that area, and these call later upon the parents and leave birthday cards. Families may be assigned pews in the nave and the first part of the service held facing them. After the baptismal promises, the procession is formed to march to the font, a server or acolyte leading, the priest next, then the parents and godparents, family by family. After Baptism,

the procession returns with the cross and crucifer leading, signifying that those baptized have now entered into the fellowship of Christ's soldiers and servants. In
one English diocese the parents, carrying the child,
follow the priest to stand at the altar rail. He takes
each child in turn, holds it up before the altar saying,
"All life comes of Thee, O Lord God," while the parents respond, "And of Thine own do we give to Thee."
Then all return to their places and the service continues
as usual. These and other methods are used to emphasize the importance of Holy Baptism. In some places
names are publicly added to the Font Roll and the
baptized prayed for by name on the Sunday after.

Private Baptism. In cases of illness, Baptism may
be administered by any baptized person, using water
and the form, "N., I baptize thee in the Name of the
Father, and of the Son, and of the Holy Ghost. Amen."
Then the Lord's Prayer and the Baptismal Thanksgiving should be used. Such Baptisms ought to be promptly reported to the parish priest, and the child or person
so baptized brought later to the church for the remainder of the service, as the Prayer Book directs.

Conditional Baptism. When there is doubt concerning the validity of one's baptism, the form prescribed
for such cases should be used. Many religious bodies
have peculiar methods of administering so-called Baptism, such as using rose petals instead of water.

Fees and Offerings. Many families like to make an offering at the time of Baptism. It should be made clear that there are no fees or charges. If an offering is made, the pastor may accept it for some special work, such as the children's corner in church or the Font Roll.

Font Roll. After Baptism little children are not to be forgotten, but suitable persons ought to keep the Font Roll, distribute leaflets to young parents, remember birthdays and anniversaries, and assist in having special services for parents and small children. There is real value in a service for parents and little children on a Sunday afternoon in June, and in the Christmas season. Some parishes have a Christmas Eve service in the late afternoon, when little children can visit the crêche in their Church, and hear the Christmas story told by their minister.

✝ 3 ✝

Confirmation

*Wherein I receive . . . the strengthening gifts of
the Holy Spirit.*
—BOOK OF COMMON PRAYER, p. 291.

A young man who lived in New Jersey, member of a
local church, had never heard of Confirmation until
he was seventeen years old. He discovered that the
"Laying on of Hands" was spoken of in Hebrews 6:1, 2
as one of the "Principles of the Doctrine of Christ" and
that the Baptism of the believers in Samaria was in-
complete without the "Laying on of Hands" by the
Apostles. He found also that the Christian Church for
fifteen hundred years had maintained this sacrament of
Confirmation by the bishops, as successors to the
Apostles. He learned that certain religious bodies at the
Reformation, having given up the succession of bishops,
had adopted various substitutes for Confirmation. This
young man resolved to do something about it for himself and inquired how he might obtain this Apostolic
blessing and be confirmed. He traveled to Philadelphia
and was confirmed in old Christ Church. Then he re-

solved to study for the ministry of the Episcopal Church and spent fifty years presenting hundreds of young people and adults for Confirmation.

Bible, History.   According to Jewish custom, a boy, having passed the age of thirteen, became "a son of the Commandment" or "of the Torah." He was regarded as able to undertake personal observances of the Law. St. Luke tells us that the boy Jesus, after passing his twelfth birthday, was taken up to the Temple by his parents. Among Jews today, the ceremony whereby a boy takes upon himself the observance of the Law is called Confirmation. It is evident that there was among Christians from the days of the Apostles a similar ceremony or custom. This "Laying on of Hands" would follow immediately or soon after Baptism in the case of adults. The Eastern Orthodox Church still follows this custom even with little children. In the Anglican Communion and in the Roman Catholic Church, Confirmation is administered by the bishop to adults and to young people who are supposed to have come to years of discretion.

Age for Confirmation.   There is much difference of opinion concerning the proper age for children to be confirmed. Some favor an early age of eight or nine years, while others think the middle or late teens better. Many think that twelve is best for the average, perhaps with the example of Christ in mind. It seems best to require proper instruction and understanding and to judge each case on its merits. An exact rule is dangerous. An elderly judge came to a certain rector, saying that he had been prepared for Confirmation in Belfast, Ireland, but was not allowed to be confirmed because he lacked one month of twelve years. The family left for the United States. Nearly sixty years elapsed between the first preparation and the judge's Confirmation.

Instruction. The task of recruiting and training young people and adults for Confirmation should go on throughout the year. Not only the clergy, but all active members of the parish should be alert to discover and interest candidates for Confirmation. Each rector will have his list of unconfirmed adults, whom he will reach, at least annually, by parish call and letter. Many persons, considered hopeless because of repeated refusals to become communicants, have finally responded when the clergy have persevered.

Courses of Instruction. Many excellent courses have been published in book and pamphlet form. The Offices of Instruction in the Prayer Book mark out five great subjects: the Covenant, the Faith, Christian Duty, Prayer, and the Sacraments. The preparation of the mind should give the basic facts of the Christian life. The preparation of the heart should provide an understanding and appreciation of the worship, symbolism, and customs of the Church. It helps to take small groups on a pilgrimage about the Church, so that many things can be seen and explained. The preparation of the will might include an act of personal dedication and the adoption of a simple rule of life. It has been found helpful for the clergy to have a personal interview with each child, asking him to come to the rector's study or office, assuring him of continued personal interest, leading him to make a pledge or resolve to be faithful, and ending with a prayer and blessing. Such interviews have great influence in young lives. All courses of instruction ought to include practice in the use of the Prayer Book, especially the service of Holy Communion.

Confirmation Classes. In many parishes, classes are held for children during the eight to twelve weeks before the bishop's visitation. These may be on Saturday morning, on Sunday afternoon at 4:30 or 5:00, or on a weekday afternoon. Regular attendance should be required and all absences made up by extra work. It is helpful to have each child keep a Confirmation notebook with written answers to important questions, facts about the Church, pictures of the bishop, the rector, the parish church, etc. These books may be displayed for the bishop and the congregation to see on the day of Confirmation.

Adult Instruction. The parish program of Christian education is planned with the thought of giving instruction to all men and women in the worship and ways of the Church. Courses of sermons on the Creed or the sacraments are especially helpful, and will be welcomed by older members, as well as by newcomers. During Advent, Lent, and other seasons there may be discussion classes in the parish house or the rectory. In some parishes in England the clergy go to homes in different areas, to which the men and women of that neighborhood are invited. The parish library will, of course, include books of instruction about the Church, which the clergy may lend to unconfirmed adults. Despite the amount of time required, careful, personal instruction ought to be given to all persons who are to be presented to the bishop.

Confirmation Sponsors.   In an ideal situation, the baptismal sponsors would be the ones to encourage a child to be confirmed and to guide him to become a faithful communicant. As a matter of fact, however, in many instances even the parents are rather indifferent to the child's spiritual development. The custom is growing throughout the Church to have Confirmation sponsors appointed by the rector. These must be faithful communicants, perhaps vestrymen or Church School teachers. These are asked to attend the Confirmation service, to make the first Communion with the new communicant, and to take special interest for at least one year. Bishop Chase of Ripon, England, has told of the custom of having a sponsor or witness stand behind each person at Confirmation. When the bishop lays his hands on the head of the child, the sponsor or witness puts his hand on the shoulder. Since this Confirmation is followed in Ripon immediately with a parish Communion, the sponsor then comes to Communion with the new communicant. This plan of Confirmation sponsors is very effective in preventing the lapse of many soon after being confirmed. It also gives definite assignments for prayer and service to lay people, enabling them in a most practical way to do effective personal work.

Corporate Communions. It is helpful to invite members of a Confirmation class to make corporate Communions in Advent and Lent. Communion breakfasts in the parish house are useful in bringing together in fellowship those who have been confirmed together. One person in each class is chosen to be chairman or secretary to assist the clergy in keeping records, to send out notices and do follow-up work.

Lay Ordination. Dr. Francis J. Hall (*The Sacraments,* p. 41) has pointed out that Confirmation closely resembles the laying on of hands with prayer in the ordination of the clergy. "Confirmation was treated by the Apostles as a kind of lay ordination, not confused at all with ministerial ordination, but somewhat analogous to it. And St. Peter's description of Christians in general as constituting a royal priesthood may reasonably be understood as presupposing their reception of Confirmation." All authorities agree that too much is loaded today upon the shoulders of the clergy. The priesthood of the laity needs to be stressed, not to infringe on the duties of the clergy, but so as to employ the great reservoir of spiritual power for the strengthening of the Church.

✛ 4 ✛

Public Worship

*My bounden duty is . . . to worship God every
Sunday in His Church.*
—Book of Common Prayer, p. 291.

Purpose.　The main purpose of the parish church
is to provide opportunities for the worship of God.
The parish at worship is the gathering of the faithful
in the community, meeting in fellowship to bear witness to their faith and to offer the sacrifices of praise
and prayer to God through Jesus Christ. The chief responsibility of the parish priest is the conduct of the
services of public worship. Of these, of course, the
most important is the Lord's own service of the Holy
Communion. As Dom Gregory Dix has said, here at
the heart of Christianity is a service of absolute sim-
plicity—the blessing, breaking, and giving of bread
and the blessing and giving of a cup of wine, as these
were done by One in Jerusalem with His friends long
ago. He asked that this be done henceforth, and for
century after century, all over the world, His friends
have done this in remembrance of Him. Despite differ-

ences of ritual and varieties of names—Lord's Supper, Eucharist, Mass, Holy Communion—this is the great service of worship for all Christians.

Hours of Worship. In past decades the average Anglican parish had Holy Communion in the morning at 7:30 or 8:00, Morning Prayer and Sermon at 11:00, with the Holy Communion celebrated on the first Sunday of the month at 11:00 and on all festivals. Evening Prayer was at 4:00, or 6:30, or 8:00. In recent years Evening Prayer has almost vanished from the Sunday worship of the average parish in the United States. In many places, however, emphasis is being placed upon a Parish Communion at 9:00 or 9:30, making this the one great service of the week. This hour seems to fit the needs of many families and it is likely that a new pattern of worship is now developing.

Methods of Worship. No priest should accept a call to a parish unless he is willing to carry on the services along the general lines to which the people are accustomed. Change should be made slowly and only after due instruction and explanation. Much harm has been done and people alienated from the Church because some zealous priest has made violent changes without proper preparation. If there is only one parish in a community, a definite attempt should be made to meet the different spiritual needs of various people. In

one New Jersey parish there is an early celebration with
no special ceremony, an elaborate service with music
and incense at 9:30 a.m., and plain Morning Prayer
with a sermon at 11:00. Many rectors give a short address at the early service, limiting it to five or seven
minutes. This is appreciated by those who prefer this
hour for worship and usually results in larger attendance. In some places young children, not yet confirmed,
kneel beside their parents at the communion rail, receiving a blessing from the priest. Also in some parishes the bread and wine to be used in the service are
brought forward at the offertory by representatives of
the congregation. The clergy should avoid all man-
nerisms and personal eccentricities. The words should
be spoken clearly and not mumbled or muttered. The
priest should memorize such parts as he speaks facing
the congregation. No rector has the right to change
the words or phrases of the Prayer Book to suit his
taste. The proper place for special prayers is immediately after the Creed, and not before the Blessing. The
service should not be prolonged by unnecessary pauses
nor should it be hurried. If a Preparation is said by
priest and servers, it can be done in the sacristy, or before the altar a few minutes before the time set for the
service. When there is a choir, there can be singing
during the Preparation. This prevents an awkward
pause when things, not heard or understood by many,

are being said before the altar. Communicants should be instructed to receive Communion with open, up- lifted, ungloved hands and to guide the chalice with the base. It is difficult for the priest to administer the chalice without assistance from the communicant, es- pecially if a large hat is worn by a lady.

Intinction. Although not mentioned in the Prayer Book, the custom of administering by intinction is authorized in many dioceses and has been recognized by recent General Conventions. There are, however, two provisos: first, that a bishop having jurisdiction may authorize intinction; secondly, that the chalice be not withheld from any communicant who desires to receive in the usual way. The Liturgical Commission reported to the Convention of 1952 that three methods are commonly used: (A) *Intinction by the communi- cant, either in the common cup or a special chalice;* (B) *Intinction by the priest, with wafer placed to the lips;* (C) *Intinction by the priest with wafer placed in the hand.* Method A is recommended by the Commis- sion, provided that a small, shallow chalice is used. If the communicant dips the wafer in the large chalice, there is danger of dipping too far. The Commission re- gards Method C as least desirable. Intinction is neces- sary where there is contagious disease, as in some places where there is much tuberculosis. It is advo- cated in many places to save time and to meet the prejudice against the common cup. When services are not unduly prolonged and the chalice is administered carefully, the cup being turned and purificators used, there is no urgent demand for intinction.

Ablutions. The majority of opinions have understood the rubric to mean that the proper place for the ablutions was after the Blessing. Recently the number of clergy who *tarp,* or take the ablutions in the Roman position, has increased. Whether this is done immediately after the last communicant has received, or after the Blessing, it should be done carefully and reverently. If the quantity of consecrated Bread or Wine be too great to be consumed at the Ablutions, the priest may leave it on the altar covered with a white cloth or place it in the tabernacle. After the service, adult communicants may then assist the clergy in reverently consuming what remains. In no case should the consecrated elements be thrown out or poured away. In some parishes there is reservation, so that the clergy may go to the sick and shut-in communicants to administer communion. It is usual to have a red light burning before the altar to indicate that the sacrament is reserved.

Candles. The custom of having candles upon the altar has become almost universal and is even common among many Protestant bodies. Two lights teach us that Christ is the Light of the world as Son of God

and Son of Man. They are called Eucharistic Candles
because they are always lit during the Eucharist.
Placed on each side of the cross they teach us that
Christ has caused the Light to shine throughout the
world by His Cross. Three candles together symbolize
the Trinity; a group of five indicates the five sacred
wounds; six lights remind us that our worship here is
imperfect, while seven is the perfect divine number,
symbolic of the sevenfold gifts of the Holy Ghost and
of the seven lamps burning before the Throne in
Heaven (Rev. 4:5). Candles should be extinguished
by the priest or a server at the end of the service. In
some places this is done during the recessional hymn,
avoiding the long pause or delay while the congregation
waits for the server to finish.

Children's Eucharists. The best way to teach children how to understand and appreciate the service of
Holy Communion is to have from time to time a service in which there is teaching and explanation at intervals. This may be done by one of the clergy while
the other celebrates, or by an informed layman who
will stand or kneel in the central isle. Unlawful omis-
sions and changes are, of course, to be avoided, in the
interest of the teaching value of the whole liturgy. Even
children can understand the difference between "shall"
and "may" in the rubrics.

Corporate Communions. During Lent, and at

other proper times, it is helpful to have members of parish organizations, such as the vestry, Church School officers and teachers, Brotherhood chapters, women's groups, as well as Confirmation classes, make their Communions together in the fellowship of their group. There is real spiritual gain in kneeling together before the altar. In one parish, where there had been much dissension, the whole atmosphere was changed after the custom of frequent Corporate Communions was instituted. Communion breakfasts with guest speakers have proved valuable.

Evening Communions. Although the institution of this great sacrament took place in the evening, the Christians of the early Church, especially among the Gentiles, made the Holy Communion the first order of business on the Lord's Day. It was thought fitting and proper to receive fasting, rather than after an evening meal. Some parishes, however, have held an evening communion on Maundy Thursday to commemorate the institution of the Lord's Supper, while others prefer to make this a preparation service for the Easter Communion. Recently the Bishop of Michigan in a pastoral letter recommended that the Holy Communion be celebrated on the evening of Saints' Days before a parish supper. Roman Catholics also have authorized evening communions to meet special needs, enjoining however, a four hour fast before such a service.

The Parish Communion.   In many places there is a movement to abandon eleven o'clock as the proper hour for Sunday worship and to stress a Parish Communion at 9:00 or 9:30 a.m. This hour is neither too early nor too late, so that whole families can worship together. As a part of the revival of liturgical interest, several new features have marked this service. The Gospel Procession, in the past reduced to the server carrying the book from one end of the altar to the other, now has become a restoration of the old symbolism of carrying the Gospel to the people. There may be a procession with the cross and tapers to the pulpit or chancel steps, while the Gradual Hymn is sung. Also at the Offertory both the alms and the bread and wine are carried forward by members of the congregation. This symbolizes the offering of ourselves and of God's gifts. Furthermore, in some places the old custom of having the priest face the people during the celebration has been revived. In some churches, a temporary altar has been set up in the nave, so that the people may gather around the altar for the common meal of this great act of worship.

Morning and Evening Prayer.   The Prayer Book expects that these services be held daily and all clergymen of the Church of England are pledged to say these offices daily. It is a mistake for the clergy who value supremely the Holy Communion as the great service of worship to neglect the Daily Offices. Morning and Evening Prayer ought to be held in every parish Church every Sunday. Many persons have been brought up to love the prayers and canticles of these services and to gain much from the reading of the two Bible Lessons. Many overburdened rectors have discovered that lay-readers are available and willing to hold these services daily, giving an opportunity for regular weekday worship. Special intercessions may then be offered for birthdays, anniversaries, as well as prayers for the sick and bereaved. In large parishes, where there is more than one priest, it is possible to have a daily celebration of the Holy Communion at such an early hour that school children and those going to business may attend. Then there may be Morning Prayer at 9:00 and Evening Prayer at 4:00 or 5:00, giving the opportunity for worship to many who now have increased leisure. Evening Prayer might well be said by young men in high school. Thus worship is seen to be a regular part of daily living and not just for Sunday.

Family Worship. In some places it has been the custom once a month to have the entire Church School attend the 11:00 a.m. service with their parents, making it a Family Service. In some English parishes there is a quarterly Parish Communion when there are five Sundays in the month. This is held at 9:00 a.m. and everyone is expected. Sometimes, as previously described in the Parish Communion, an altar is set up in the nave, the celebrant faces the people, and the elements for the consecration are brought forward with the alms. In these English parishes one housewife represents all the housewives by bringing forward one wheaten loaf to the altar. One of the men, an elected representative of the congregation, brings forward the flagon of wine, purchased by the gifts of the people. As all these are presented, the clergy and people join in saying a prayer of thanksgiving and dedication. Intercessions are offered before the Prayer for Christ's Church. Thus emphasis is placed upon the united worship of the parish as one family in God.

✦ 5 ✦

The Forgiveness of Sins

The forgiveness of sins, according to the riches of his grace.

—Ephesians 1:7.

The Problem. The fact of sin is recognized by all. The statistics of juvenile delinquency and the cost of adult crime stagger the imagination. No one can possibly reckon the damage sin does to human welfare and happiness. Early in the history of the Christian Church the need to repent, to confess one's sins, and to find forgiveness was counted an imperative for health of mind and soul. In many of his Epistles, St. Paul is shown as a pastor dealing with the sins of the congregation. Every minister of Christ has the problem of dealing effectively with the facts of sin. Due to advances in psychology, the destructive results of moral guilt on mental health are clearly recognized today. Psychiatrists have rediscovered the law that catharsis, the cleansing of the mind by confession, brings release and health.

The Gospel. The good news of the Gospel has been and is the proclamation of divine forgiveness for all who truly repent. The death of Christ upon the Cross is set forth as "the full, perfect, and sufficient sacrifice, oblation, and satisfaction for the sins of the whole world." The sacrament of the Body and Blood of Christ is celebrated as the "perpetual memory of that his precious death and sacrifice." Here the Christian pastor has a mighty force not available to the psychotherapist as such. Christ lifted up on the Cross moves men to repent, makes possible forgiveness, and His holy institution enables those who confess their sins to be cleansed by His grace, to be incorporated into His mystical Body, and to continue in that holy fellowship.

Public Confession. From the earliest times confession of sins has been a part of public worship in the Christian Church. In theory, if not always in practice, the self-righteous Pharisee has always been condemned, the penitent Publican forgiven. At first individuals were expected to confess publicly before the congregation; later on, privately to the bishop or priest. At the Reformation the private confessional was abolished by most of the new denominations. Always, however, there was informal confession to the pastor, or to the elders and deacons. Dr. Harry E. Fosdick once said that he had heard innumerable confessions in his office. Public confession of sin by the congregation remains the rule in The Book of Common Prayer of the Episcopal Church, in the Lutheran Churches, and other liturgical bodies. All are required to confess that they have offended, that they have left things undone, and done things which they ought not to have done. Then, in the Episcopal Church, the priest, or the bishop, stands and solemnly pronounces the Declaration of Absolution.

Private Confession. Such public confession as above may be made personal if each penitent comes prepared after self-examination to make a real act of contrition. Many persons, however, who are burdened with guilt, find such a general confession inadequate. The rule of the Anglican Communion is that all persons *may* make private confession to the priest, some *should* do so to find release and victory, none *must* be required or compelled to make a private confession. All clergy, however, are expected to be prepared and ready to hear private confessions and to administer, if requested, the sacrament of Penance.

The Place. The Church, of course, rather than an office, is the proper place for the priest to meet those who wish to make a formal, sacramental confession. The priest should be seated, wearing his vestments, with a purple stole, either inside the communion rail or in a pew near the back of the nave. The penitent can then kneel at the rail or in a pew behind the priest. If a kneeling desk is provided, the priest may sit in a chair near by. The west end of the church, rather than the sanctuary, is by tradition the proper place for the confession of sin. No recognition is given between priest and penitent during the confession or afterwards. No reference is ever to be made and the seal of secrecy is absolute. The priest does not even look at the penitent. Of course, if a confessional box is provided, these details are cared for.

The Preparation.   To hear confessions and to help penitents requires preparation. The need for pastoral counseling is widely recognized among Protestants as well as Catholics. Every priest should prepare himself spiritually and intellectually to meet the needs of his people. He should teach the difference between true contrition, sorrow for sin as grieving our Lord, and regret at the consequences of evil. He will show methods of self-examination and make available to all booklets that teach and explain the way of penitence and forgiveness. Those who desire to make a private, sacramental confession need to come prepared, after self-examination, to mention all sins remembered since the last confession. One rector, being told by a lady that she had no special peace or joy in her religion, suggested that she make a complete examination and then a confession. She exclaimed in surprise that she had nothing to confess. However, she went back in thought over her life and found many things amiss in thought, word, and deed. After confession, there was for her a wonderful peace and joy from the forgiveness of sins.

The Form. The following form for private, sacramental confession is suggested:

> *Penitent:* Bless me, Father, for I have sinned.
>
> *Priest:* The Lord be in thy heart and upon thy lips, so that thou mayest confess all thy sins: in the Name of the Father, and of the Son, and of the Holy Ghost. Amen.
>
> *Penitent:* I confess to Almighty God, the Father, the Son, and the Holy Ghost, and to you, Father, that I have sinned exceedingly in thought, word, and deed, by my fault, by my own fault, by my own grievous fault, especially I accuse myself of the following sins:
>
> *(Confession may be read from notes; no unnecessary details; no names mentioned; habitual sins indicated.)*
>
> . . . .
>
> For these, and all other sins I cannot remember, I am heartily sorry, firmly purpose amendment, humbly ask pardon of God, and of you, Father, penance, counsel, and absolution.
>
> *(After questions, counsel, an appropriate penance may be given in the form of prayers or psalms. These are acts of devotion, not a payment or satisfaction for sin.)*
>
> *Priest:* God Almighty, have mercy upon you, forgive you your sins, and bring you to everlasting life. Amen.

The Almighty and merciful Lord grant you pardon, absolution, and remission of your sins. Amen. Our Lord Jesus Christ, Who hath left power to His Church to absolve all sinners who truly repent, and believe in Him, of His great mercy forgive thee thine offences; and by His authority committed unto me, I absolve thee from all thy sins, in the Name of the Father, and of the Son, and of the Holy Ghost. Amen.[1] And the blessing of God Almighty, the Father, the Son, and the Holy Ghost be upon you, and remain with you always. Amen.
Go in peace, for the Lord hath put away all thy sins. Amen.
(The penitent rises, kneels elsewhere to perform the penance assigned, makes an act of thanksgiving, and goes away with peace and joy.)

Counseling. There is new recognition among all Christians of the need for, and the value of, pastoral counseling. Many persons realize that there is something wrong in their lives and they feel the need of talking it over with someone. The inner pressure of guilt compels them to find relief in telling their inmost secrets to one who will listen without being shocked, who will keep their confidence inviolate, and who will give helpful counsel. In sacramental confession the very fact of the penitent coming to confession is evidence of sincerity and the priest sits in the place of spiritual authority. In pastoral counseling, however, the pastor tries to guide the conversation so that the person will

[1] From the English Prayer Book.

see clearly his problem, understand the situation, and make his own decision. The wise parish priest will prepare himself to serve in a dual capacity, as friend and counselor, listening to the troubles of his people, and as representative of the great High Priest, giving with authority the declaration of absolution.

✛ 6 ✛

Christian Marriage

Those whom God hath joined together.
—Book of Common Prayer, p. 303.

Holy Matrimony. The family is the fundamental institution of society. Upon the ideal of a permanent, lifelong union between one man and one woman have been built the Christian family and the Christian home. From this ideal there has come the moral discipline of manhood, the elevation of womanhood, the recognition of the responsibilities of parents. The structure of a civilization worthy to be called Christian must rest upon Christian marriage. The supreme sanction of Holy Matrimony is given in the words of Christ: "Those whom God hath joined together, let no man put asunder."

Preparation. A couple came to a rector to be married, listened to him speak about the meaning of Christian marriage, whispered privately to each other, and then said that in view of his words they had decided not to be married. He was amazed, but later the girl telephoned, said they had acted hastily and were quite unprepared. Three months later they returned and were, after instruction, united in Holy Matrimony. This illustrates the fact that general preparation ought to be given in any parish, so that young people will know the meaning of marriage, learn how to choose partners wisely, how to avoid the obstacles and over-come the difficulties in the way of successful marriage. In some places an annual sermon is preached, usually in June, on Christian marriage, and all married couples, especially those married in that parish church, are urged to attend. It is helpful to have talks given in young people's groups about dates, petting, courtship, and marriage. Sometimes a forum meeting in Lent can deal with the subject of Christian marriage. One par-ish makes this an annual event, with various authori-ties as speakers and with questions from the floor. In the Diocese of New Jersey in 1955 the subject of the summer conference of young people was preparation for Christian marriage. Every parish ought to have good books on marriage available for young people and engaged couples.

Interviews. When a couple comes to a clergyman to make an appointment for a wedding, he must, of course, see that all legal requirements are fulfilled. Full information must be obtained as to birth, age, names, addresses, Baptism, previous marriage if any. The license is to be in the hands of the priest as soon as possible, and not at the last moment. One Church wedding had to be cancelled on the day before, because the bridegroom concealed his divorce and held back the license.

Instruction. If several interviews are possible, there will be instruction in the meaning of Christian marriage as distinct from the legal union. The minister will speak of marriage as a partnership entered into reverently, a union blessed by God through His Church, and the establishing of a family and home where Christ is a living Presence. The teaching of the marriage service in the Prayer Book will be studied and the symbolism explained. Such matters as the giving away of the bride, the public taking of each other by handclasps, the ring ceremony, the prayers, and the blessing, all will be considered and understood.

Sex. Fortunate is the pastor who can refer a couple to a Christian physician who can give a general examination, sex counsel, birth control information, and afford the opportunity to ask questions. It is usually not advisable for the clergy to give sex information, although they may speak of the physical, as well as other aspects of Holy Matrimony, in a simple and natural way to remove any sense of guilt or misconceptions.

Difficulties, Problems. Many family feuds are caused by money troubles, so it is helpful to have the couple discuss this with the pastor. Property, income, savings, allowances, debts, charge accounts, insurance, joint checking accounts—all these are matters which may cause real conflict. It is well to have each person resolve to put the other absolutely first and to permit no relatives to interfere. Many a marriage has gone on the rocks because mother's wishes, rather than those of husband or wife, have prevailed. When two persons belong to the same church or have similar faiths, they will be reminded of the importance of worshipping together, having family prayer, and grace at meals. When there are serious obstacles in religion between them, these should be set forth clearly, overcome if possible, and the convictions of each respected by the other. The greatest difficulty is in the case of Roman Catholics and Protestants, because of the insistence of the Roman Church that such marriage is not truly valid unless performed by the Roman priest, after a pledge by the Protestant to have children brought up in the Roman faith. Constant bickerings over Church often result and religion becomes a source of discord rather than a bond of union. Relatives interfere and pressure is put upon one or the other to abandon convictions and accept the other faith. Of course, if one party is strong in his or her principles, and the other has only a nominal religious membership, it is logical for them to unite in one Church. Because it is both Catholic and Protestant, the Episcopal Church has frequently proved the solution and the Church home for many couples. In any case, they should be advised to work out a solution before they are married. Dean Pike's book, *If You Marry Outside Your Faith,* is most helpful.

Rehearsals.   Weddings should be held in church if possible and a rehearsal is desirable. It is good to give a short instruction to the whole wedding party before the rehearsal, to teach reverence for the Church and understanding of the service. Ushers and bridesmaids need to be told their duties and where to stand. No secular music is permitted. Suitable fees for organist and sexton are expected. Picture taking during the ceremony is prohibited, but arrangements may be made for posing for photographs after the service. The rector, and not any social director, is understood to be in full charge of the marriage service. The priest has the right to refuse to conduct any marriage.

The Service.   It is evident that the Prayer Book service of Holy Matrimony is intended for Christians who are baptized and who intend to contract a valid and permanent marriage. Before the service the couple are expected to sign a Declaration of Intention to this effect. Communicants may desire to have a nuptial celebration of the Holy Communion immediately after they are married. In this case, the couple and their attendants remain kneeling at the communion rail after they are pronounced man and wife, the priest goes to the altar to begin the celebration, the couple receive first, and then relatives and friends, and the marriage blessing is given just before the Benediction.

Blessing of Married Couples. Some couples who have been married by secular officials later desire the prayers and blessing of the Church. In some countries a secular service is required by law before a religious ceremony. Full information is necessary before consent is given to perform such a service for a couple already married. In all doubtful cases the facts ought to be presented to the bishop and his judgment obtained. On wedding anniversaries, especially Golden Weddings, the clergy are frequently asked to conduct a service. It is proper to use parts of the Prayer Book service and to have the couple renew their vows.

Annulments, Divorces. When a marriage has been declared null and void by the state, the Church accepts this decision and regards the person as one that has never been married. When divorced persons ask to be married, the parish priest explains first, that considerable time is required in all cases for the facts to be presented to the bishop for his judgment. Only when there are grounds for holding the previous marriage invalid and not a true marriage, should the parish priest burden the bishop for his decision. If there appear to be such impediments as consanguinity, mistaken identity, lack of free choice, insanity, impotency, perversion, disease undisclosed, fraud, or duress, there is the possibility that the bishop may rule that the couple may be married by the parish priest. The responsibility for judgment and dispensation rests upon the bishop or the ecclesiastical authority of the diocese or district in which the person is canonically resident.

The Banns. In many places today there is an effort to stress the parish fellowship, and to make all members interested in welcoming those who are baptized, confirmed, or married in the parish church. The publication of banns, according to the Prayer Book rubric and the custom of the Anglican Communion, enables all parishioners to know of the prospective marriage and to act accordingly. Where the parish group system is used, persons living in that area may later arrange a social evening when the new couple may be guests of honor. This means much in deepening parish fellowship and holding young married people to active membership in the church.

+ 7 +

Ministering to the Sick

I was sick, and ye visited me.

—St. Matthew 25:36.

Opportunity. Sickness opens the door of opportunity for the Christian pastor. As shepherd of the flock he is responsible to minister to his people in times of sickness, for they greatly need the comfort and healing power of God. All persons are more open to spiritual influence in times of sickness, including the one who is ill and those about him. When forced by illness to stop and lie in bed, many, who have been indifferent to religion, have done serious thinking. Often they are ready to make a change and build a new life. The pastor who is alert and faithful in visiting the sick will discover many opportunities. The minister who neglects the sick suffers loss far greater than he can realize.

Notice of Illness. Too often people take for granted that their rector knows of their illness and they wonder why he does not call. Congregations need to be admonished of their duty to notify the clergy promptly, so that prayers and visits are possible. With some effort a parish can be trained to telephone the parish office to send word of illness in the family or neighborhood. Even if he already knows, the rector will thank people heartily when they send word. In some places group leaders are appointed to gather such information and keep the pastor up to date.

Attitudes. There are pagan and there are Christian attitudes toward illness and affliction. By word and example the minister of Christ will teach that disease is never God's will, that God is not the author of disorder and weakness, and that Christ never went about making people sick, but was the Good Physician to heal and comfort those who came to Him in faith. Physicians and surgeons do marvelous work, but are not infallible. Miracles of healing do take place. There are no limits to God's power. In a true sense, there are no hopeless cases. We must trust God absolutely for this life and beyond. There are obstacles that prevent healing; unrepented sin, false ideas, destructive fears. The healing power of a living faith, the dynamics of prayer, the need for spiritual growth; all these are to be preached and taught to prepare people for sickness and sorrow. In some parishes the Sunday nearest St. Luke's Day (Oct. 18) is used for a special service of "Religion and Healing." Doctors and nurses are invited. The Bible Lessons may be read by hospital officials. Missions of spiritual healing have proved their value in many places.

Preparation. The clergy will prepare themselves to visit the sick. Without knowledge of the patient, effective pastoral work is not possible. The essential facts are needed in each case. Inquiries may be made of the family, the doctor, the nurse at the hospital desk. Cases have been known of clerical malpractice, when a patient who appeared well, but was near death, heard only jokes and jolly remarks from the uninformed visitor. The pastor will prepare himself spiritually to go as the representative of Christ. His mind will be furnished with prayers memorized and with Bible passages at his command, for it is better to give these from the heart without a book. He will prepare himself physically, making his person clean and neat, with no offensive odors. His voice at the bedside will be strong, but not loud; natural and easy, but not ecclesiastical or official.

The Visit. As a general rule, all visits to the sick will be brief, ten minutes or less. Many sick persons cannot endure long visits and their recovery is hindered. In critical cases a brief message of hope can be given, prayer offered and a blessing. Of course, there are cases of convalescence when longer visits are desirable. At times the patient needs to talk, to find release in speaking to one in confidence, and the pastor will do well to listen. It is helpful to keep a notebook, to record dates and the main theme stressed, such as "Faith," "Love," "Trust." Thus one can come with a different message no matter how often the calls are made. Sometimes a spiritual prescription can be left on a card for the patient to take so many times a day. If the sick person is anxious, this may be an act of trust with a Bible verse to repeat. Pictures, leaflets, prayers may be left at the bedside and often prove valuable. Flowers from the church are appreciated, but not by those critically ill. One parish sends flowers with this message:

> These flowers are from the altar of St. Barnabas' Church. They bring you a message of the Peace of God's House and the assurance that you are remembered in the prayers offered there.

Holy Communion. Devout communicants will request the parish priest to bring them the Sacrament. If the numbers are not too great, the short form in the Prayer Book will be used. The special Collect, Epistle, and Gospel on page 322 of the Prayer Book may be used, or, especially if the Sacrament is administered often in a long illness, those for the proper day. An altar can be set up on a table or bureau. Cross and candles can be brought by the priest. Every parish should have a portable communion set. It is possible to wear a cassock, to roll it up under a coat, and to have a small stole in a pocket. Parish priests should encourage their people to have services of the Holy Communion in their homes.

Reserved Sacrament. In many cases it is necessary to administer by the Reserved Sacrament. The priest will place the Sacrament in a pyx to be worn about his neck or in some proper receptacle in the pocket of his cassock. He will keep silence except for urgent necessity. When he arrives there will be no ordinary conversation, but the service will be held at once with the Confession, Absolution, Prayer of Humble Access, Communion, Lord's Prayer, Thanksgiving, and Blessing. In some places administration is in one kind only and in others intinction is used. When intinction is the custom, the priest should dip the wafer and place it in the mouth of the sick person. In critical cases the service as above may be shortened still further.

The Laying on of Hands. In accordance with the example of our Lord and Apostles, many pastors use the laying on of hands when visiting the sick or at services of spiritual healing in the church. Various forms are used. Bishop Conkling in his book, *Priesthood in Action,* suggests the following as preferable for general use to the one in the Prayer Book:

> I lay my hands upon thee in the Name of the Father, and of the Son, and of the Holy Ghost; beseeching the mercy of our Lord Jesus Christ, that all pain and sickness being banished from thee, the blessing of health may be thine.

At St. Stephen's Church, Philadelphia, where a notable ministry of spiritual healing is carried on, the Rev. Dr. Alfred W. Price holds two services every Thursday, at which scores of persons come to the altar rail for the laying on of hands. Many persons afflicted with all sorts of diseases have been healed.

Unction of the Sick. Provision is made in the Prayer Book for this ministry to those who "shall in humble faith desire the ministry of healing through Anointing." The priest dips his right thumb in the oil and makes the sign of the cross upon the forehead, as in Baptism, saying:

> I anoint thee with oil, In the Name of the Father, and of the Son, and of the Holy Ghost; beseeching the mercy of our Lord Jesus Christ, that all thy pain and sickness of body being put to flight, the blessing of health may be restored unto thee. Amen.

Persons should be instructed before receiving Holy Unction to confess their sins, to have humble faith and trust, but not to think an immediate miracle is guaranteed. In some dioceses the bishop blesses oil for this purpose on Maundy Thursday. It may also be obtained through various guilds.

Intercessions. Many parishes have prayer groups of those pledged to offer intercessions for the sick. At St. Stephen's, Philadelphia, nearly one hundred intercessors are enrolled, who receive a list of names with special needs. Prayer is offered daily for these for a month or six weeks. Parish priests would do well to encourage this practice. Many elderly, shut-in persons find inspiration in praying for others, but need guidance. Instruction in intercessory prayer can be given in sermons, talks to parish groups, and in private.

Operations.   A certain lady, told by her doctor that she must have a serious operation and that he could not guarantee favorable results, fainted away in the office and had a nervous collapse. Many suffer from anticipation and fear of an operation. The clergy can help much by teaching faith in God, trust in the skill of the surgeon, so that quiet confidence may prevail. Sometimes the pastor may visit just before the operation and give a blessing. More frequently he can assure the patient that, at the very time of the operation, he will be there in spirit, offering prayers and intercessions.

Death.   Even when medical authorities have abandoned hope, the Christian pastor will maintain his faith and confidence. One rector, told that a man could not survive two hours, administered Holy Communion by request of the patient. The next morning the man sat up and ate a hearty breakfast and within a week was back at work. The physician expressed amazement, saying that some new factor had come to give an impulse toward health. All Christians, sick or well, should be prepared to pass through the gate of death. The faithful go with faith and confidence, knowing that God will do better things for them than are possible in this imperfect world. When death appears imminent, the pastor often remains to strengthen and comfort all by his presence. The dying may wish to make confession or to express last wishes. Even if unconscious or in a coma, sick persons frequently are aware of prayers and blessing. Seldom, however, does the pastor speak of death. His emphasis always is upon life, life eternal, and victory through Christ.

✛ 8 ✛

The Ministry of Sorrow

In the confidence of a certain faith.

—BOOK OF COMMON PRAYER, p. 317.

Death.　If rightly instructed, people will notify their pastor promptly when death comes to a family, and he will go at once to comfort and strengthen the bereaved, and to arrange for the services. He comes as a friend, as a man of God, and as one who knows what is fitting and proper for Christian burial. No faithful pastor will delay or leave matters to the undertaker. No arrangements should be made until the clergy are consulted.

The Church.　For all baptized persons the church is the proper place for funerals. Prayers may be said in the home, but an overcrowded house or a public funeral parlor cause more strain and tension for the bereaved than the church. In the church are familiar surroundings, the symbols of the Christian faith, and proper facilities for caring for many people with dignity and reverence. Organ music is available and hymns may be sung. Relatives may enter at a side door to sit at the front. They may follow the casket out or may leave by the side door. Some may even prefer to remain in the vestry room during the service. A pall to cover the casket may be available. Since this is for all alike, it signifies God's mercy upon all. In some places the Church's Flag is used as a pall, just as the American Flag is used at military funerals. The casket must always be closed at church funerals.

Flowers. A great display of flowers is to be avoided in church. There may be flowers upon the altar and, if no pall is used, upon the casket. The custom is growing for families to request friends to send no flowers, but rather make a memorial gift to some worthy purpose.

Music. The rector, if the family desire, will arrange for suitable music, suggesting to the organist appropriate hymns and organ selections. If there are vested singers, they may take their places quietly in the chancel before the service. If there is a crucifer and vested choir, they may go down the side aisle with the clergy to meet the casket, and then up the center aisle preceding the casket. After the service, the choir may remain in their seats or go down the center aisle. At the recessional the clergy immediately precede the casket. No person should come between the clergy and the casket. Pallbearers carry the casket or follow. The

Nunc Dimittis or Psalm 130 may be said or sung during the recessional or a hymn played softly.

The Service. Complaints are made that the clergy depart further from the Prayer Book in the conduct of funerals than in any other service. Strictly speaking, no rubrical permission is given to use any prayers except "such other fitting prayers as are elsewhere provided in this Book." Bishops, of course, have the right to use and authorize special prayers and devotions. Many lay people much prefer the familiar words of the Prayer Book, rather than poems and prayers from other sources. Psalms 39 and 90 are suitable for the aged; Psalm 27 for the devout; Psalm 130 when there is bitter sorrow; Psalms 46 and 121 are for all. The great Resurrection Lesson is best for teaching, while the shorter Bible selections speak of comfort and hope. The Apostles' Creed is always to be used. At times it is advisable to say, "Let us stand and express our faith by saying the Apostles' Creed." Some clergy prefer to conclude the service with the Commendation and Commendatory Prayer (Prayer Book, p. 319) or with the devotions known as the Absolution of the Body. The body of a lay person is to be placed at the head of the nave with the feet toward the altar. The body of a priest is taken into the chancel aisle, facing the congregation, with the head nearest the altar.

The Committal. If this is to be said in church, the

priest will leave his stall to stand directly before the casket. During the committal prayer earth or sand, not flowers, will be cast three times upon the casket, the pall or blanket of flowers being folded back. This may be done by the undertaker or by the minister himself. At the cemetery, the clergy always precede the casket to the grave and stand at the head for the service. In cases of cremation the committal service, whether held at the place of cremation or later at the grave, is the same. There is no official objection to cremation in the Episcopal Church.

The Closed Casket. It is the universal rule that the casket be closed during and after the service in church. It is strongly to be recommended that this rule be followed for all funeral services, whether held in funeral parlors or in homes. When this is not done, there is the emotionally disturbing scene of mourners bidding a last farewell to the body after the uplifting and comforting words of the service have been spoken. Constant and regular instruction will in time, it is hoped, do away with this unfortunate situation.

Funeral Fees. It should be made clear that the clergy do not charge fees for their services. The undertaker is not to be permitted to include such a charge on his bill. If, however, the family wish to make an offering as an expression of appreciation for services rendered, the minister may accept it for himself or his discretionary fund. If there is music with an organist or soloists, proper compensation will be made. No charge is made for the use of the church. If the deceased and family are not members of the parish, it would be fitting that an offering be made for the church.

Burial of a Child.   The Prayer Book provides a service for children, but specifies no ages. As a rule the Office for the Burial of a Child will be appropriate for those children who have not been confirmed. It is proper, of course, for the clergy to use parts of both Offices for burial. White, rather than black or purple, is the color for the burial of children.

Fraternal Services.   When the burial ritual of a fraternal order is to be used, it is better for this to be done on the evening before the church service, or after the completion of the burial service at the grave.

Requiems.   A Collect, Epistle, and Gospel are provided in the Prayer Book for the celebration of the Holy Communion at a funeral. Some families prefer to have this in the early morning with the public funeral later in the day. When the Burial Office and the Requiem Celebration are held together, the priest will use his best judgment as to what is fitting. Frequently the Creed is omitted from the celebration, either because it has been said previously or to signify that the departed has passed from faith to knowledge. The *Gloria in Excelsis* is also omitted. Usually only the celebrant and server make their communion, though sometimes the immediate family do so. At the request of the bereaved, with the thought of the Communion of Saints in mind, Requiem Eucharists may be celebrated on All Souls' Day, November 2nd, and on the anniversary of a death.

Memorials. Many persons desire to do something in remembrance of loved ones, but are prevented by the expense. From time to time, the clergy will, through the parish papers and various announcements, let it be known what things are needed in the parish buildings which would make suitable memorials. For example, a parish office might be refurnished in memory of some active worker; the Kindergarten room might be equipped in memory of a child; new hymnals or chant books might be given in the name of one who loved music. In many parishes a Book of Remembrance has been dedicated, so that any person may start a memorial fund in the name of a loved one, by the gift of any sum from one dollar upwards. No announcement is made concerning amounts given, so that rich and poor are alike share in this opportunity. Names of donors are placed in The Book of Remembrance on the same page on which the date record of the departed is made. Some person, perhaps the rector, will act as trustee and treasurer. Gifts will be placed in a savings bank and invested for the support of the church. Such gifts become permanent memorials to strengthen the church. A record of dates will enable the clergy to remember with prayer at the altar all names in The Book of Remembrance, on the anniversary of death or on the Sunday nearest. Once a year, on All Saints' Day, or the Sunday nearest, a memorial service will be held for all so remembered in the parish. When notice is sent to relations and friends, many will attend and will desire to add further to the memorial funds.

The Bereaved. Death in a family always affords an opportunity for the priest and pastor who loves his people. Grief softens hearts and makes them responsive. Kindness in time of sorrow makes a deep impression. Pastoral works of comfort, faith, and hope give the sorrowful strength for the present and courage to face the future. Sometimes the pastor helps most by saying little, but standing by with the attitude of confidence in God. The wise pastor will let people talk out their grief and not repress their sense of loss. He will not try to cheer the sorrowful with easy words, but speak of thanksgiving for good years past, of fragrant memories, of loved ones promoted to better things beyond this imperfect world, and of the sacred duty of carrying on as he or she would wish.

+ 9 +

Christian Vocations

*Every member of the same in his vocation and
ministry.*

—BOOK OF COMMON PRAYER, p. 590.

Divine Vocations.   It has always been the belief of
Christians and the teaching of the Church that God
has a plan and a vocation for every member. At Baptism we are pledged to continue Christ's faithful soldiers and servants unto life's end. For each one God
has a plan, a work to be done, a place in life where
service can be rendered most effectually. Some find
their true vocation early; some may do so later on in
life; some are frustrated and hindered so that they accept a secondary calling in which to do their best. Always there is service to be rendered, a ministry to be
performed, and that is our vocation.

The Apostolic Ministry.   Christ called the Apostles
to leave all to follow Him, that they might be trained,
empowered, and commissioned to be the chief ministers of His Church. He also called the seventy elders

73

or presbyters to go out as His ministers and evangelists. Later on, seven deacons were ordained to be assistant ministers. From the time of the Apostles there
have been these three orders, Bishops, Priests and
Deacons in the Apostolic Ministry. This is the highest
vocation, the greatest privilege for any man, to serve
as devoted entirely to God, to stand at the altar as representative of the great High Priest, to administer the
sacraments, to preach and teach the Word of God. No
one is worthy of this honor. None should enter this
ministry unless truly called of God. Yet there is need
for clergy, parents, faithful communicants to present
this call to young men and boys, to magnify this office, to set forth this life of adventure, devotion, difficulty, and spiritual reward. It is, of course, a high
honor for a family to have one of their number in holy
orders. Parishes which produce no young men for the
ministry ought to be ashamed. All congregations who
are informed about the life and work of the Church
will give generously to the annual offering for theological education. They will also take an active interest
in helping young men to be trained for this ministry.

Priesthood of the Laity. From Apostolic times it
has also been the teaching of the Church that every
member has a priestly character, that there is a real
priesthood of the laity. The priest at Holy Communion
never celebrates alone. He acts with and for the people.

When a child is baptized, the minister acts both for Christ and for the congregation, saying, "We receive this child." Confirmation may be presented as the ordination of the laity, which, if rightly understood, may help one to know what St. Peter meant when he spoke to the people as "lively stones, . . . a spiritual house, an holy priesthood, to offer up spiritual sacrifices, acceptable to God by Jesus Christ" (I Peter 2:5). There is a ministry and service for all God's people, not at all in conflict with the duties of the clergy.

Perpetual Deacons. Devout laymen, not called of God to give up their profession or business, may serve in the Church as perpetual deacons. This requires study and preparation. Examinations must be passed. The bishop and the standing committee must be satisfied. After such men are ordained deacons, they may render valuable service even though their ministry is limited. The number of perpetual deacons is rapidly increasing, but the Church could use many more of them. Many large parishes would be greatly strengthened and overburdened rectors relieved when there are many communions, if such a deacon was available.

Missionaries. In the Mormon Church every young man is expected to go out as a missionary at his own expense for several years. It would be helpful in every Church if the call to serve as a missionary and evangelist was given to all. Then reasons would have to be found by those unable or unwilling to accept this service. Great opportunities are evident in such foreign fields as Japan, the Philippines, Cuba, Liberia. In such fields as Alaska, the Hawaiian Islands, Puerto Rico, the Canal Zone, and Brazil there is need for teachers, secretaries, doctors, nurses, and practical business men to serve the Church.

Deaconesses. The Order of Deaconesses provides opportunities for women to be set apart with limited vows to serve God and the Church in an official capacity. Deaconesses wear a uniform, qualify by special training, and have great value in pastoral work and religious education.

Religious Orders for Men. The Church has always had a place for those who, like St. Paul, have been called to remain unmarried and free from family ties to serve God in special ways. Monastic orders offer a vocation with vows of poverty, chastity, and obedience. In the Episcopal Church there are a number of orders for men, both clergy and laymen, among the best known being the Order of the Holy Cross and the Society of St. John the Evangelist (Cowley Fathers). The names and addresses of all of them are given in the Episcopal Church Annual.

Religious Orders for Women. Likewise from early times there have been in the Church, Sisterhoods for women who are called to the monastic life as their vocation. The vows are also of poverty, chastity, and obedience. There are fifteen such orders for women listed in th Episcopal Church Annual. Many of them are doing a notable work in deepening the spiritual life of the Church, in maintaining schools for girls, and in assisting parish priests. The Community of St. Mary, for example, has an excellent school for girls at Peekskill, N. Y., a convalescent hospital for children at Bayside, N. Y., a retreat house for men and women in New York City, a school and mission among the mountaineers of Tennessee, as well as several schools in the Midwest and on the West coast.

Church Army. This evangelistic and missionary society of the laity was founded in England in 1883 and extended to the United States in 1927. A uniform is worn; men are commissioned as captains; women are known as sisters. Salaries are paid. Some of the captains are married. Much has been accomplished by the Church Army in the United States, but much more might be done if their number of trained workers was increased.

Women Church Workers. The Church maintains two official training schools for women workers: Windham House in New York, which in 1952 combined with the Church Training and Deaconess House of Philadelphia; and St. Margaret's House in Berkeley, Calif. There is great need for young women to be trained to serve as deaconesses, directors of religious education, parish secretaries, church workers on a full time basis. There are business and administrative positions under the National Council, in diocesan and missionary fields, in Church Schools, and in large parishes.

Vocational Guidance. It is the high privilege of the parish priest to give vocational guidance to his people. He will, of course, encourage all to serve in various parish activities, from serving at the altar to working in the kitchen of the parish house. But at suitable times, both in public and in private, he will present the different varieties of Christian vocations. Many young people drift into various jobs without any knowledge that the Church has fields of Christian service. The Church can be presented as God's Highway, the means of following our Lord in our several vocations. It would transform life for many persons, if they had a true sense of vocation, if as parents, business men and women, laborers in various ways, they could offer to God their ministry and service. This teaching can be done at suitable times during the year, such as the Epiphany season, the Annunciation, Labor Sunday, St. Matthew's Day, St. Andrew's Day, and the third Sunday in Advent.

✛ 10 ✛

Pastoral Calling

I am the good shepherd, and know my sheep, and am known of mine.

—St. John 10:14.

Door Bell Ringing. Some have been heard to say that they do not waste their time in ringing door bells, and that people know where the church is and should come to the clergy. Others point out that modern conditions make pastoral calling difficult. Many young pastors are inclined to make no real effort in regular pastoral calling. Richard Baxter at Kidderminster used to set aside days for calling and would announce on Sunday the families to be visited and the schedule of calls. Interviews with each person would be held and instruction given. Then family prayers would be conducted for the whole household. Only in places where the Family Day plan is used is there now even a remote approach to this pastoral care of the past.

Importance. If, however, a man intends to be a real pastor, a shepherd of the flock, pastoral calling is a "must." Christ Himself visited in the homes. He was an honored guest in many places, and thus people came to know and trust Him. Only when a man gets to know people can he be a true pastor. Only when people feel their minister to be a real friend, sincerely interested in them personally and individually, can they go to him as guide and counselor. Pastoral calls must be made. Nothing can take the place of them in an ordinary parish. One may have the gift of eloquence and shine like a Chrysostom in the pulpit, but without the knowledge of people in their homes and the understanding of conditions under which they live and work, the power of the sermon will be largely lost.

Priority. Every pastor will know and teach his people the order of importance in his pastoral visiting. First of all he must go to the sick, especially those critically ill. Nothing alienates a family more than to have their rector delay and postpone his coming in cases of serious illness. Nothing strengthens the pastoral relations more than to have the man of God come promptly and regularly to bring courage, hope, and blessing at such times. And nothing is more irritating to the clergy than to have people fail to notify him, to suppose that he knows, and then to be grieved at his absence. Only constant instruction to a congregation concerning the importance of notifying the pastor can prevent this.

Emergencies. Next in order of priority will be

cases of emergency or crisis. If word comes that an only son has been killed in an accident; if a home is about to be broken by divorce; if a man has been discharged unjustly by his employer after years of faithful service; if another has been arrested and charged with some offense; all these constitute emergencies for families and individuals. They are opportunities for the pastor to bring the power of the Gospel to uplift and change life. Prompt action will mean much; delay often causes failure.

New Families.   In growing communities where new families are moving in continually, the zealous pastor will be alert to reach them promptly with an invitation to share in the worship and fellowship of the church. Prompt calling makes a deep impression on the newcomers. Delay often means that the children go to other Sunday Schools and the family is lost to a more active religious body. Hence the pastor will encourage his faithful people to notify him of new families and he will visit them as promptly as possible. Through real estate agents, by the help of "The Welcome Wagon," and other community means, he will keep himself informed of names and addresses.

Regular Members.   Last in order of priority will come the faithful and regular members of the parish. They should be told that the sick, the emergencies, and the new people come first. But they need assurance that their pastor is always available to them in any case of need. In the average parish every family will be visited at least once a year. In small parishes calls can be more frequently. Special difficulties exist in large city parishes with many apartment houses. Even there, however, a regular plan of pastoral visiting by the rector and his assistants will be effective.

Call Books, Records. It is expected that a good parish will keep a complete card index of all families and individuals. There will be accurate addresses, information as to Baptism, Confirmation, communicant membership, transfers, birthdays (at least for young people), marriages, and deaths. Without such an index, constantly corrected and kept up to date, the work of the pastor is greatly hindered. A good parish secretary, paid or volunteer, can render invaluable service. One of the purposes of regular parish calling is to secure information so that records can be maintained. Notes can be made on small cards before the call. Additions and changes can be written during and after the visit. Many pastors find a calling book helpful in which all families are placed according to districts and streets. If a man finds himself making a sick call on a certain street or in an apartment house, he can look in his book and see what other families are in that vicinity. Of course the date of the call will be recorded.

Calling by Lay People. Many men in the ministry

fail to use the parish resources available to them in their own people. This is especially true in parish visiting. Lay members will not make calls indiscriminately on their fellow members. They will, however, when assigned calls for definite purposes, go and accomplish much. One rector makes a rule to follow many of his calls by an assignment to one or more of his active members. If it is a new family, he writes his request on a form card and mails it to several suitable families in that neighborhood. Guild or auxiliary members are asked to call and invite the new lady to their meetings. Vestrymen are requested to call and invite the new couple to sit with them in church or to attend a parish dinner as their guests. Very definite results are obtained by this method. When there is sickness that is chronic and long continued, the rector can enlist the aid of persons to take flowers and make friendly calls. When there is need to secure workers for a parish project, teachers for the Church School, a leader for the Y.P.F., the Scouts or the Camp Fire Girls, the pastor can ask one or two persons to go with him to make the call. Such a delegation makes a real impression. When two or three men walk in, it is harder to refuse the call to service than if the rector calls by himself. In some parishes, once a year, lay people are enlisted to call on every family, not for finances, but simply to promote friendliness and encourage activity.

Purposeful Calling. Many persons think of parish calling in terms of aimless ringing of door bells. This seems to accomplish nothing and to degrade the minister of Christ into a cheap salesman. The answer to this is purposeful calling, visits that are planned and have a definite goal. One pastor makes a habit of diagnosing each family to consider what their needs are. Are they new people who need more friendly contacts? Are they faithful ones who just need encouragement and appreciation? Is there an unbaptized child or an unconfirmed adult? Do the communicants come regularly or are they lax? After careful thought and prayer, the rector sends letters, expressing his appreciation for faithful attendance, for medals in Sunday School, good work in organizations, etc. Search is made for something to be commended and appreciated. Then the rector points out tactfully something that troubles him, saying, for example, that he is concerned to see this communicant so seldom, or he is troubled because this name is not on the list of workers or givers. The letter concludes with an expression of friendliness and the intention of calling soon. When calls do follow such letters, the results are immediate and gratifying. Faithful ones are delighted to know that their service is noted and appreciated. Inactive persons are touched by such a personal message and the concern of the pastor. The follow-up of such purposeful calling is important. Notes

are made and the information acted upon without delay. If a desire is expressed to share in some parish
work, word is sent to one of the officers. If there is an
unbaptized or unconfirmed person, the name will be
placed on the rector's prospect list.

Anniversaries. Another fruitful source of purposeful calling is found in birthdays and anniversaries. It is
not difficult to make a calendar index with a card for
each day of the year. One can then enter names of
those born on that day with the year, if available. Marriage dates, especially those performed by the pastor,
can be easily recorded. Some busy clergy enlist volunteer secretaries to keep this file up-to-date and to give
him notice of approaching anniversaries. It is easy to
see that a call on a wedding anniversary or a birthday
has a special meaning and value. Even a telephone message or a brief letter will tell the parishioner that their
pastor has a special thought for them on that day.

Family Day Plan. At the Cathedral in Garden
City, Long Island, N. Y., and in other places, families
have been asked to select one day in the year that has
special meaning for them. It may be a wedding anniversary, a birthday, or any convenient date. They are
told that prayers will be offered for that family in their
church on that day and that one of the clergy will call
at the home. In many instances the family go to the
service and make a special effort to be home when the

clergy call. This plan makes possible the kind of pastoral calling that used to be common in the nineteenth century. When daily services are not held, a modified form of this plan can be arranged so that intercessions are offered on the Sunday nearest the date, or at one of the weekday services.

Blessing the Home. In some parishes it is a custom to invite the clergy to visit a new home to offer prayers and blessing. Suitable prayers are available for the rooms of the house. Children have been encouraged to set up prayer corners or little sanctuaries with a religious picture, a cross and candles, Bible and Prayer Book. This may be very simple and the end of a bureau or bookcase may be used. One rector announced he would gladly come to dedicate such home sanctuaries. As a result there was a revival of home religion and family prayers. Some young people took pride in making their own crosses and candlesticks. Dr. E. A. Hunter, Methodist pastor of Wichita Falls, Texas, had printed a certificate of dedication to be framed and hung in homes that had been blessed.

Pastoral Kit Bag. Just as the family doctor takes on his calls a black bag with various useful remedies, so the physician of souls will go to the homes provided with suitable materials. The effectiveness of a pastoral visit is enhanced when one leaves behind, at the bedside or in the home, cards with comforting messages, leaflets that teach, spiritual prescriptions to be taken so many times each day. When calls are made on new families, it is helpful to leave copies of parish bulletins or service leaflets. One rector found it useful to have with him a book of pictures showing parish life and work. New people are impressed when they see photographs of the congregation coming out of church, the choir marching in procession, the Church School, the men's Communion Breakfast, etc. One veteran pastor always carries a supply of sweets, life-savers or something similar, which are welcomed by children and many adults. Children flock about him wherever he goes and his Church School is overcrowded. Many of the clergy have found persons glad to contribute to the replenishment of the pastoral kit bag. Often when the rector calls and no one is at home, the calling card with something from the kit bag will impress the family, make them aware of the church, and frequently bring them to worship the next Sunday.

✛ II ✛

The Rector

Thy servant to whom the charge of this Congregation is now committed.
—Book of Common Prayer, p. 572.

Responsibility.   Each parish is a miniature of the whole Church, a Christian community worshipping and serving together. The real work of the Church is done through the parishes. Thus there is laid upon the rector, by the canons and customs of the Church, a very heavy responsibility. All services of worship must be planned and directed by him. His spiritual jurisdiction covers the entire parish. Subject to the canons and rubrics of the Church, and the godly counsel of the bishop, the burden of leadership and direction is his.

Powers.   According to the canons, the rector is given powers to meet this responsibility. He has the control and use of the church and other parish buildings. He is given authority in all matters of worship; even the selection of hymns and anthems come under

88

his jurisdiction. He may invite others to take part in the service or may forbid them. He can organize or disband any parish organization except the vestry. He has sole authority over the Church School and the religious training of children. He can forbid and refuse the Holy Communion to a wrongdoer, even to the extent of announcing names to the congregation (Prayer Book, p. 85). He is the official head of the parish corporation, presides at vestry meetings, appoints committees, and presides at the annual meeting of the congregation.

Call. When a rectorship is vacant, the vestry are empowered to elect and call a man, subject to the advice and consent of their bishop. Usually a committee is appointed to receive and consider names and to make a recommendation to the vestry. In some dioceses the bishop nominates one or more persons for first consideration, and then, if these are rejected, makes further nominations. It is not good form for a priest to make application himself. The call is complete when in writing the vestry invite a man, the approval of the bishop has been received, and the man in writing accepts the call. The amount of salary and other perquisites are to be stated clearly in the call. Usually the bishop approves the choice of the vestry unless he has very definite and strong objections. In some dioceses, however, the bishop by canon and custom exercises much authority and influence in the choice of men for rectorships, forbidding the consideration of men not nominated by him.

Institution.   It is an old custom, not a rule, that a new rector be duly "instituted" by the bishop according to the form in the Prayer Book. In this impressive service the senior warden, or some other representative, presents the keys of the church in token of acknowledging the rector's control and jurisdiction. In response the new rector promises to be a faithful shepherd and, kneeling at the altar, pledges devotion to his duties and asks for grace and power from God to meet his responsibilities.

Tenure of Office.   A man is called and instituted as rector, not for any term of office, but for life. He cannot be forced to resign, except for definite charges as provided by canon. Although elected by the vestry, he is regarded as a priest of the whole Church, a representative of Christ, not as a local employee of the vestry or congregation. It requires at least a year for a man to become acquainted with his parish and people. It is therefore a mistake for the clergy to become restless and move about from place to place without staying long enough for real achievement.

Rector and Parish.   The rector is in the parish as shepherd of souls, with a divine commission to be a pastor for all the people. His authority is from above. His priesthood is primary. Although he functions as legal and canonical head of the parish, his principal aim is to be the servant of Christ and the minister to the souls committed to his care. He does not think of the parish as his in a possessive sense, as a place where he can act in an arbitrary fashion to carry out his own notions. His first consideration is the spiritual welfare of those now looking to him as their rector and pastor.

Rector and Staff. If there are paid or volunteer members of the parish staff, it follows that they work under the direction and authority of the rector. Curates and assistant ministers, by whatever title they are known, must serve under the authority of the rector, even though their salaries are set by the vestry. Every clergyman who assists a rector is expected to be loyal to him, refusing to make criticism or to allow himself to be used by any faction or troublemakers. Much harm is done when a popular young curate allows disaffected parishioners to use him to spread discord in the parish. He does not have to agree with all the rector's decisions, but he can keep his criticisms to himself and resign when he can no longer work loyally with his superior. The choirmaster or organist must also serve under the rector's authority, following his suggestions, since by canon law the control of church music is given to the rector. Such must also be the case with the parish secretary, director of religious education, and the sexton. Team work is important. The wise and tactful rector

will not try to be a petty dictator. He will consult fully
with those who are expert in their fields and appreciate
their gifts and abilities. Blessed is that parish where the
rector understands how to use his authority wisely and
well, without such arbitrary actions as cause irritation
and complaint. No radical changes in worship or organization ought to be made without careful consideration, proper explanation, and the hearty co-operation of most of those concerned.

Rector's Family.   The wife of the rector is expected
to be in sympathy with her husband's work. She is not,
however, employed by the parish, nor should she be
expected to have authority or responsibility beyond
that of any faithful member. It is usually better for her
not to accept any office or chairmanship in the parish,
but to stand ready to assist and serve in special ways.
The same is true of other members of the family of the
rector. Some fortunate men gain greatly from the criticisms and suggestions of their wives. Others have been
hindered in their ministry because the wife has tried to
run things in the parish or has talked too much about
people.

The Diocese.   Because he is not just a parochial official but a priest of the Church, the rector has a responsibility to share in the life of the diocese or missionary district. He will see that the parish register and
other records are so carefully kept that reports will be

made promptly and accurately to the diocesan office. His presence is expected at diocesan conventions and clergy conferences. His bishop depends upon his loyalty and interest to see that the local church shares fully and actively in the life of the diocese.

The General Church. Members of a parish are always tempted to be parochial in outlook, to think of the Church primarily in terms of their local place of worship. It is the duty of the rector to present the whole program of the Church, to preach and teach the meaning of the worldwide redemptive fellowship, so that missionary support will be regarded as a privilege. It is an established fact that support of the local church is never injured by giving to outside projects. On the contrary all experts agree that the missionary-minded parish will always be stronger and more active at home than the parochial congregation.

Rector's Report. Bishop Slattery, when rector of Grace Church in New York, used to require every member of the staff to make a monthly report, showing services conducted, sermons and addresses, baptisms, marriages, burials, parish calls, meetings. Some rectors keep such a record for themselves and require it of their assistants. One new rector gave his report at the first vestry meeting and his men expressed great astonishment at the amount of his work. Many of them evidently still had the old idea that the clergy had little to do except on Sundays. By request the report was printed in the parish bulletin and much favorable comment resulted. Regular reports such as this accomplish much in lay understanding of the work of the ministry.

+ 12 +

The Vestry

There are differences of administrations, but the same Lord.

—I Corinthians 12:5.

History. The election of wardens and vestrymen to serve as custodians of church property and representatives of the congregation is a comparatively new thing in Church history. In the early days of the Church of England, except in a few instances, there was no such body as a vestry. Parishioners, when convened for parish business, were described as assembled in vestry, because they usually met in the room where the clergy put on their vestments. In the American colonies, such as Virginia, Maryland, and New York, at an early date parishioners were authorized by law to elect men to be vestrymen to serve as trustees and perform other duties. The present vestry system in the American Church is modeled after the custom which began in England, especially in London, to have a representative body called a "select vestry."

Constitution. According to law, the vestry in most dioceses is composed of the rector, *ex officio,* two wardens, and a number of vestrymen, varying from six to twelve. Most parishes are incorporated under the Religious Corporation laws of the state under the name of *The Rector, Wardens and Vestrymen of* .... *Church.* These three together compose the vestry. This system affords a combination of spiritual leadership and representative democracy which is unusual. In the Roman Catholic Church the lay people have little power over church property, while the clergy control both spiritual and financial affairs. Among many Protestant bodies the elected boards of laymen may act without the pastor, for he has usually no right to preside or to be counted as a member of the board.

Election. Every parish is required to have an annual meeting, duly announced according to law, at which usually one warden and one-third of the vestrymen are elected by votes of qualified members of the parish. The rector presides, judges the qualifications of voters, (or appoints judges to do so), receives the ballots, has them counted by tellers, declares men duly elected. In some dioceses, such as Pennsylvania, the rector's warden is appointed by the rector and the accounting warden (treasurer) is elected by the vestry. Both wardens and the majority of the vestrymen (all if possible) should be faithful and active communicants. The qualifications of voters at parish elections vary according to state and diocesan laws. Usually a qualified voter is a baptized member, over twenty-one years of age, who has attended the parish church and contributed to its support during the previous year. There ought to be in each parish a list of those baptized or confirmed in that parish or transferred to it.

Annual Meetings. Instead of having only a few present for the annual election, many parishes have made the annual meeting an interesting and notable gathering. There may be a parish supper, followed by an address by a capable speaker. Interesting dramatic reports may be made by parish organizations. Financial figures, for example, may be presented in large cardboard pictures or graphs. The annual canvass may be depicted by a dramatic skit in which one man interviews another. The Woman's Auxiliary may show their activities by teams of ladies demonstrating worship, study, supply, fellowship teas, etc.

Vestry Meetings. As a corporate body the vestry is charged with the responsibility of the finances and the maintenance of the church property. Without such material resources the parish cannot function properly. The rector, as presiding officer, will see that the vestry is properly organized at the first meeting after the annual election. He will take care that meetings are held regularly and promptly and necessary business speedily transacted. If this is done, there will be time for information and discussion beyond that of bills to be paid. Vestry meetings may have a spiritual significance. If the salary of a curate is to be voted, the problem of pastoral care may be discussed. If funds are needed for some Church School project, the rector may lead a discussion on religious education. The wise and tactful rector maintains his own prerogatives, but also uses vestry meetings to secure the understanding and support of the laymen chosen by the congregation. It is possible, as one alumnus wrote to a seminary dean, "to be canonically right but practically wrong."

Committees. Much of the detail which plagues some vestry meetings can be avoided if the committee system is used. All petty matters should be handled by the proper committees so that only important questions are presented to the vestry. Committees should report regularly and make definite recommendations. In one parish the rector asks each committee (finance, property, education, music, hospitality) to study the situation and to present a complete report at one assigned meeting during the year. It is helpful to give each chairman an exact statement of the duties and responsibilities of his committee. In some large, well organized parishes, such as Christ and St. Michael's in Philadelphia, each member of the vestry is given certain definite assignments and duties for the year.

Powers.   All matters of finance and property come within the jurisdiction of the vestry. They serve as trustees of the property of the parish and are expected to maintain and repair the buildings and grounds. The rector controls the use of the church and other buildings for religious purposes. The delivery of the keys at the Office of Institution is symbolic of this authority. In one parish the vestry were opposed to the rector admitting non-white persons to the services and locked the door against the rector. Their action was illegal and futile. The powers of the vestry are corporate, not individual. They must act at regular or special meetings, duly called, and a quorum must be present. The sale and mortgaging of church property is usually not permitted without the consent of the congregation, the bishop, and the standing committee of the diocese.

Property.   The title to church property is usually vested in *The Rector, Wardens and Vestrymen* as a corporate body. It may, however, be vested in a board of trustees, a diocesan foundation, or even in the bishop as a *Corporation Sole* (Chicago). Many dioceses, realizing the need for guidance in the erection of church buildings, have commissions on church property. These may approve or disapprove plans for new buildings, suggest changes, supervise insurance. There are also diocesan committees on financial safeguards to see that vestries have proper systems of audit and bonding of those who handle money, reports, and insurance. From time to time parishes do suffer great loss because of inadequate insurance, dishonesty of officials whose books were not properly audited, and mismanagement of endowments.

Auxiliary Vestry. In parishes where a broad construction is given to the vestry, as an official parish organization for lay participation in all aspects of parish life and work, it has been found useful to have an auxiliary vestry. This is a body without legal status, composed of persons (usually men, but women may be chosen), who are elected or appointed by the rector and vestry. They may meet regularly or occasionally with the vestry. They have no vote on strictly legal matters, but may be given a voice and vote on all other parish affairs. In one large suburban parish there are two wardens, twelve vestrymen, and twelve auxiliary vestrymen, the latter being chosen annually by the vestry. The auxiliary vestrymen meet with the vestry, serve on committees, learn the business of the church, and are naturally available when election of regular vestrymen takes place. This plan gives a parish a large number of informed, active men and enables a newcomer to break in and be tested. This system is recommended when the rector wishes to make large use of the available man power in his parish.

Rotation. Many parishes have adopted the *ro-*

tating vestry plan to change a static situation. One rector came to a new church and found every member of the vestry over sixty years of age and learned that most of them had served more than thirty years. The plan to change this should be adopted by resolution at an annual or special meeting of the congregation, after ample discussion and explanation in advance. It is then decided that no vestryman be re-elected after his term expires until one year has elapsed. If the vestryman be a key person, such as the parish treasurer, he may continue to serve as treasurer and attend meetings, without being legally a member of the vestry for one year. If the auxiliary vestry plan is followed, it is easy to keep valuable men in touch with affairs. The rotation system enables inactive men to be dropped without hard feelings and gives new men a real chance.

Honorary Officers. It has happened in many places that a warden, for example, has served faithfully for many years, but now is unable to attend regularly to such duties. No one wants to ask for his resignation. Yet his absence makes quorums difficult and his inability to serve hinders progress. The solution is to elect him an honorary warden at the annual meeting. with the privilege of attending meetings whenever possible. His name is retained on parish bulletins as an honorary member of the vestry. In similar situations other parish officials may be made honorary.

Installation. To give dignity and recognition to the elected representatives of the congregation some parishes have adopted the Vestry Installation Service. On the Sunday after the annual election (or another appropriate date), all the members of the vestry march forward to the chancel steps. The rector conducts a brief service in which they pledge themselves to serve faithfully; he declares them duly elected and installed and gives them his blessing. One California parish calls this Vestry Recognition Day and invites all former wardens and vestrymen to be present.

Parish Council. When a parish has a large number of organizations, it is helpful to have a parish council composed of representatives from the vestry and from each organization. Meetings are held quarterly or at the call of the rector. Such a body affords the opportunity to consider plans and policies for the whole parish, to send back information through the council members to each society, and to obtain opinions quickly concerning any proposed action.

+ 13 +

Parish Finances

Every man shall give as he is able.

—Deuteronomy 16:17.

The Church and Money. According to Abbé Michonneau in his book, *Revolution in a City Parish,* the chief obstacle for the Church is the belief that religion is nothing but a business affair, that all priests are after money, and that the Church is just another racket. This opinion, justified or not, does exist in certain circles. Many pastors in their calling have had people take for granted that they are out for contributions. Constant appeals for money during services of worship and numerous money-raising activities in parish houses cause many to associate religion with the clink of money.

Stewardship. It is obvious that the worship and work of the Church cannot be carried on without money, any more than government, schools, or homes. Taxes are paid up on incomes and property in due proportion. Definite instruction ought to be given to all

Christians to develop principles of stewardship, ideals of trusteeship, and a sense of personal responsibility for time, talents, and treasure. These will be presented throughout the year, not only in sermons, but in programs of the Church School and parish organizations. Church members will then expect to give generously to God of their time and their talents, as well as their money. The spiritual significance of the Offertory needs to be explained, that men at that moment of worship may think, not just of an anthem or of money, but of the symbolic dedication of their lives to God. Perhaps more sermons ought to be preached on the familiar text, "All things come of Thee, O Lord, and of Thine own have we given Thee."

Management. To secure adequate support the church must demonstrate good management. People need to have confidence that the parish has a worthy program, a well-considered budget, suitable salaries, honest and able administration of funds. Mismanagement is almost as fatal as dishonesty. Offerings ought to be counted and recorded immediately after each service by several persons. Parish treasurers and all who handle considerable sums must be bonded. Special gifts, missionary contributions in particular, will be promptly forwarded, and in no case used improperly to pay ordinary current expenses. Bills must be paid without undue delay, so that the good name and the credit of the church will not suffer in the community. At regular times the accounts of the parish treasurer and the books of all financial officials in the parish will be audited by competent persons. This protects both the parish and the individuals concerned. No one should be subjected to the temptation of handling money without accounts being checked. There have been in the past too many instances of personal and parochial tragedies, when such business methods have not been followed.

The Rector. The chief responsibility for parish finances rests upon the laymen of the vestry. However, the leadership of the rector is a vital factor. He simply cannot disassociate himself from parish finances. By preaching, by instruction, by interesting and appointing leaders, by his own attitude and example in money matters, the parish priest exercises great influence. When things go wrong he must take action. One rector, for example, found that a trusted parish treasurer had for years handled all funds without an audit and without being bonded. When he objected, the officer took it as a personal insult and the vestrymen backed him up. When the rector persisted, despite this opposition, and diocesan authorities took a hand, it was discovered that this man had been for years taking church funds for his own use.

Canvass. Most parishes have found that an annual canvass for the support of the church's program is a necessity. When this is thoroughly done, good results are certain. In a sense, however, it should come as a natural and regular part of the church's life. The challenge for responsible giving must be presented, but the emphasis need not be solely or primarily upon money. Visitors will go out to inform and interest people, so that giving to the program of the Church will be bound to result. If people know about these things and believe in them, they will welcome the opportunity of generous support. Many weeks before the canvass, a chairman and committee are appointed, a parish survey made, a budget drawn up to show expenses and probable income, and a time schedule determined. Publicity is important. Printed matter must be prepared. Visitors are to be enlisted and trained. A master list of all possible givers requires office work. A special gifts committee has been useful in many parishes to deal with unusual cases. Tact and skill help greatly in assignment of names to visitors. The pastor's intimate knowledge may be of great value.

Loyalty Sunday.   In many places a Sunday is appointed when pledge cards, previously received in the mail, can be filled out and presented at the altar. This plan enables faithful communicants to respond promptly and reduces the number of visits that must be made. The disadvantage, of course, is that these receive no personal appeal and the visitors have only difficult calls to make. The ideal method is to have every family and individual visited and told about the latest plans of the parish.

The Follow-Up. Most parishes fail to obtain the best results because there is little or no follow-up to the canvass. Seldom is the work fully completed. Usually there are many who have not been reached with a personal invitation to share more fully in the life of the church. It is good to have in a parish a committee that functions throughout the year to follow up the canvass, to invite newcomers to use weekly offering envelopes, and to check on unpaid pledges.

Young People. Frequently the young people of the church are overlooked in the annual canvass. This is a great mistake for these young people need to be trained in stewardship for the future support of their church. Most young folks have allowances and earned income, so that they can pledge and give to the church. Some parishes have a canvass committee of young people which functions in a similar fashion to the adult committee. Visits and appeals, of course, are made by active young people upon their own list.

Pledges. The ideal is to have every member make a pledge for the program of the church, so that the vestry may know what to expect and be able to take businesslike action accordingly. When a large number refuse to pledge, but say they will give when they come to church, the total income is a matter of guesswork. All parishioners will be urged to make a pledge for the sake of the welfare of the church, with the understanding that this may be changed in case of necessity. One visitor, finding a lady obdurate in her refusal, said that he wanted her name on the list of contributors, and that therefore he would pledge one dollar in her name. This shamed her so, that she cried out that she could easily give five dollars as her pledge.

Letters, Reports.   Some parishes make great use of letters to present the needs of the church and to set forth standards of tithing and proportionate giving. Pictures, drawings, and cartoons give an imaginative presentation. Financial reports need not be dull. It helps, for example, to say what it costs to maintain the church for one day or one week. It is good to ask for a pledge of one hour's income per week. It helps to compare church giving with the cost of tobacco or other luxuries. Some parishes send monthly reports, not bills, to each contributor, showing the amount of his pledge and the sum received. Many parishes publish the list of names of contributors, but not the amounts.

Missions.   It is a mistake to emphasize the needs of the local parish to the practical exclusion of the missionary program of the Church. Over and over it has been shown that people give more to the home church when they are informed and interested in missions. The wise rector will see that the annual canvass presents the whole program of the Church in parish, diocese, nation, and world. The missionary quota ought to be taken for granted as one of the definite obligations of the parish. Some parishes find it helps to adopt a missionary or to select a mission field for special study and giving. Arrangements can be made for this through the National Council. One large parish that had failed for years to raise its quota was persuaded to adopt as its missionary, first a missionary nurse in Alaska, and later on a bishop in the foreign field. Letters and visits from these champions of the faith produced great results. The missionary cause was seen in terms of these personalities.

Money-making Activities. Too often parishes have been dependent upon bazaars, cake sales, and dinners, so that the support of the Church has been cheapened in the eyes of the general public. Far better is it to maintain the altar by the gifts of the people, and to use the parish house activities for fellowship and special needs. Rectors, however, make a mistake to abolish all bazaars and dinners. Many persons find real pleasure and friendliness in serving at such affairs so that their abolition leaves a vacuum. It is generally agreed in the Episcopal Church, and many bishops have made it a positive admonition, that there be no bingo, raffles, or selling of chances to raise money for the Church.

Talents, Pennies. Bishop De Blank in his fine book, *The Parish in Action,* describes the method of talents used in some English parishes. On an appointed Sunday, leaders of various groups come forward during the service to receive £5 with which to trade and work. During the next few months this money is used in all sorts of family and group affairs to earn larger amounts. Then on Sunday the leaders come to present the results. In the United States some parishes have raised special funds, such as The Builders for Christ quota, by giving "Joash Chests" or "Penny-a-Meal" boxes and having them used in homes and brought in to be presented at the altar on a given Sunday. Even in summer resort parishes, such as St. James, Atlantic City, this plan has proved successful. The diocese of Chicago has a "pence can" project that raises considerable sums of money for special needs.

+ 14 +

Christian Education:
The Church School

So that you may teach the people committed to your Cure.

—BOOK OF COMMON PRAYER, p. 542.

History. In a sense all real education is religious, for it arises out of the need to prepare young people for the best and fullest life, to enable them to adjust themselves to the things, the people, and the problems of the material and spiritual world. Among the Hebrews the synagogue has been a center of teaching and learning, the Old Testament being the chief textbook. The Jews were the first to provide education for all, each child being taught at home and in the synagogue schools. The Christian Church began with those whose training had been in the synagogues, so that classes for instruction of children and of adult catechumens were found everywhere, as the writings of Clement, Origen, and Augustine show. During the Dark Ages all education declined in Europe, though the monasteries continued as centers of learning. Then came the Renaissance with a revival of education, the growth of universities, the invention of printing, and the Reformation. Luther urged general education. The Jesuits formed a system of schools and instruction. Catechetical teaching became the rule among Protestants and Catholics. In England, parish schools were common, but not until 1870 did the government establish the first elementary schools. In the United States, town schools were set up in Massachusetts as early as 1647, but Horace Mann (1796-1859) is regarded as the father of the American public school system.

The Sunday School. The modern Sunday School movement is dated from 1780, when Robert Raikes, a printer in Gloucester, England, started a school for children on Sunday, and persuaded four ladies to teach reading and the Church Catechism. The school began at ten o'clock, continued till noon, met again at one, with a reading lesson followed by Church service, and closed at half-past five. Robert Raikes edited *The Gloucester Journal* and wrote articles that aroused interest, so that these "charity schools" were started everywhere, despite much opposition. Bishop William White established a Sunday School in Christ Church, Philadelphia in 1788, and became President in 1790 of The First Day Society, whose object was to establish Sunday or First Day Schools.

Importance. Today the importance of Christian education is recognized by all Christians, and the Sunday School, though much criticized for its failures, is known to be a most important part of the Church's life and work. Since the teaching of religion is excluded from the public schools of America, millions of children receive their only knowledge of the Bible and the Christian faith from the Sunday School. Too often parents teach little religion at home, but expect all to be done in the short time available to the Sunday School. One Roman Catholic priest expressed to an Episcopal rector his amazement at this, saying that, without the parochial school on weekdays, their Church would go backward in two generations.

The Rector. The chief responsibility for religious education in every parish belongs to the rector. The whole program of instruction for the adults of the congregation, for Confirmation classes, for Bible classes and forums in Lent, as well as the Church School on Sundays, is to be directed personally by the rector. No matter how busy he is, he will not abandon this to any assistants, lay or clerical. He will make his presence and words felt in every department. It is possible for the rector in large Church Schools to visit different departments and classes in turn, preparing himself so that he can speak in review of the previous lesson or concerning the lesson of the day. Thus children of all ages will know him as their rector.

Hours. It used to be common to have Sunday School in the afternoon, but social habits have changed. Most sessions now are held at 9:30 or 9:45 a.m., though many schools meet at 11:00, so that parents may attend church while the children are in classes in the parish house. The development of the Family Service and the Parish Communion has in many places shifted the emphasis from the so-called "holy hour" of eleven to a mid-morning time on Sunday when families may worship together. At St. John's, Bethesda, Md., St. John's, Norristown, Pa., and other large parishes, the largest congregation of the day is at ten o'clock.

Worship. The importance of teaching children to worship is universally recognized. When they only meet in the parish house and have brief services there, the church may seem to be a thing apart. Then there is the tendency to cease the practice of religion when they leave Sunday School. Instruction in worship may be given by having the children in church for the opening service before they go to their classes. If this is not practicable, rooms in the parish house may be fitted as chapels with temporary altars, so that the service may have familiar surroundings and teaching value. In St. John's, Lansdowne, Pa., a large and beautiful chapel in the parish house enables worship to be held without interference with the services in the church. In St.

Thomas's, Mamaroneck, N. Y., where the church stands on a hill with the parish house below, the younger children (except for special occasions) meet for worship and instruction in the parish house, while the upper grades go to the church and then to class. Once a month, however, all the children and parents throng the church for a Family Service.

Church School Communions. There is general agreement that it is good to have from time to time a celebration of the Holy Communion for the Church School, with explanation and teaching at intervals throughout the service. If there is only one priest, it is not too difficult to train a layman to be vested and placed in the center aisle to give short explanations.

Grades, Departments. It seems best to place children in classes according to their standing in public schools, rather than by age. There may be exceptional cases, but as a rule children will accept this decision without objection. Likewise, the public school divisions of Kindergarten, lower grades, Junior High, and Senior High form natural departments. In small schools two grades or more may have to be grouped. It is best, if possible, to have one competent teacher for each grade. Children are accustomed to boys and girls being together in weekday school, so many think this ought to be done on Sunday, even if the class is large and an assistant is needed.

Officers, Teachers. A good superintendent will prove invaluable to a busy rector. In one parish the rector was always present at Church School sessions, but he was blessed with two fine laymen as superintendents. One shared actively in worship, while the other attended to business matters and discipline. Another important officer is the secretary, for attendance records must be kept and supplies maintained. Perhaps the most difficult problem of Christian education is the enlistment and training of teachers. Best of all, of course, are the men and women who spend their weekdays in education, and yet are willing to consecrate their talents on Sunday to teach religion. In many instances, however, untrained but well-meaning adults have to be used in Church Schools. It helps greatly to have teacher training institutes and classes at least monthly, so that the lessons to be taught can be covered in advance. All teachers are to be encouraged to attend diocesan institutes, and to do everything possible to improve their methods. In many parishes efforts are made to dignify the office of teacher and to show appreciation. It helps, for example, for the vestry to give an annual dinner to the officers and teachers.

Courses of Study. As might be expected, there are many courses used in the Episcopal Church. The Cloister Press of Louisville in the 1940's started the Cloister Series, some courses of which, especially in the high school grades, have been revised and are now published by Morehouse-Gorham Co. The Pastoral Series was edited by the Rev. Robert S. Chalmers of Baltimore, and is published by Morehouse-Gorham, who also publish various individual courses. In the 1940's also the St. James Lessons were developed in St. James' Church, New York in the rectorship of Bishop Donegan with the Rev. Dr. Bernard Bell as editor. In the diocese of Pittsburgh and elsewhere the Pittsburgh Series of Sunday School lessons have proved their value. Many parishes have used lessons published by various Protestant Churches, choosing whatever the rector or the teachers think most helpful; but with the development of new courses in the Episcopal Church, most parishes no longer find this necessary.

Episcopal Church Fellowship Series.   The philosophy underlying this fine series is that Christian education must be God-centered, and concerned with the building of intelligent citizenship in the fellowship of the Christian community. The publishers, Morehouse-Gorham Co., have rendered a real service to the Church in making available at this time a complete series of courses from the Nursery to High School, incorporating elements of earlier series with the best of new methods.

The Seabury Series.   In October 1951 the Seabury Press was established as a publishing house, owned and operated by the Episcopal Church and closely associated with the Department of Christian Education. Under the direction of the Rev. John Heuss, D.D., and the Rev. David R. Hunter, Ed.D., the Church's Teaching Series has been published with books for adults covering such subjects as the Bible, Church History, Doctrine, Worship, and Work. The Seabury Series of lessons, after much study and research, has been produced to give the Church the best progressive techniques, to foster the child's religious development, and to show him that the Church in its Sacraments, Bible, Creed, and Ministry answers to his deepest needs. In many ways the Seabury Series is a radical departure from older lessons. Many parishes are not ready for this, for it requires much more of parents and teachers in preparation and co-operation.

Attendance.   Since the actual time for instruction in Church Schools is so limited, it is important to secure as regular attendance as possible. Many schools provide rewards for perfect attendance, including attractive pins, buttons, certificates, and honor rolls. All scholars absent more than two Sundays ought to be visited, even though this requires much effort. Some parishes use members of the Y.P.F. or the Junior Brotherhood for this.

Discipline.   Many schools have serious problems of discipline. Since the same complaint is made concerning the public schools, it is not surprising that restless, active youngsters create disturbances in Sunday Schools. The best cure, of course, is to have competent teachers who love children and can interest them. Real trouble makers ought not to be allowed to disrupt a class. It is better for them to be sent out to be cared for by the superintendent, who may assign special work for them to do in The Office of Instruction of the Prayer Book. Frequently it helps to give active assignments as clerks, monitors, and servers to boys who can hardly sit still. One such lad, deemed hopeless by many and almost expelled from public school, after a man-to-man talk with the rector, became his special clerk and assistant, and later on a crucifer and leader of the Young People's Fellowship.

Offerings, Finances. The old idea was for the Sunday School to be quite independent of the church, with the offerings of the children paying all bills. In recent times many of the clergy have realized the value of making the school an integral part of the church, so that the offerings of the children in weekly envelopes are treated the same as those of adults and the bills are paid by the parish treasurer. Missionary giving is encouraged and the Lenten Mite Box affords many opportunities for instruction. Sometimes a goal is set for the whole school and quotas accepted by the classes.

Missions for Young People. There is great value in holding every three or four years a series of afternoon services for the youth of the parish. These might begin on a Sunday afternoon, continue daily at 4:00 p.m., except Saturday, and conclude on Sunday. Fruitful results can be obtained if the missioner is competent. In some instances a large percentage of the children of the parish has attended regularly, concentrated instruction has been given in dramatic ways, and many outsiders brought in. High school young people can be used with good effect as ushers, layreaders, and choir singers.

Commencement, Diplomas.   To hold these young people who tend to drop out in the teen ages, some Church Schools offer diplomas and graduation to those who complete the tenth grade, having done previously satisfactory work according to certain standards. Parents are expected to urge their young people to graduate. Commencement is held in June with diplomas and even hoods awarded to the graduates. Crosses are given to honor graduates. Teachers who have served so many years also receive hoods. This makes an interesting and colorful ceremony.

Adult Classes, Bible Classes.   The ideal situation would be to have classes for all ages, from the Kindergarten to the Adult Class. Large Bible Classes ought to be the usual thing in the Episcopal Church. This is the Church which produced the King James Bible and the Book of Common Prayer, of which four-fifths is

Bible. This is the Church which has Lessons from the Old and New Testament scheduled for Morning and Evening Prayer. No service of Holy Communion is complete without a passage from the Epistles and the Gospels. When real efforts are made, it is possible to arouse adults to attend Bible Classes in Advent and Lent. Parents who bring children to Church School on Sunday mornings can be persuaded to attend the worship service and to remain for a Bible or discussion class. Emmanuel Church, Philadelphia has over seventy parents in such a class.

Parochial Schools. Because of the inadequacy of Christian education even in the best of Church Schools, and even when the released time program is used, many parishes have started weekday parochial schools similar to those maintained by Roman Catholics and Lutherans. Far better religious training can be given when children come daily to the parish school.

Home Co-operation. Great emphasis is placed in the Seabury Series and in the Episcopal Church Fellowship Series upon the vital importance of parental co-operation. It is easy to see, no matter what lessons are used, how tremendous is the influence of the home in religious education. When parents set examples of weekly worship and daily prayer, when Bible stories are told, religious questions discussed, and Church affairs treated as important and interesting, then children become truly educated for Christian living. When parents are careless and indifferent and merely send children to the Sunday School, the whole process of religious training is hindered.

✛ 15 ✛

Church Music

Singing and making melody in your heart to the Lord.

—Ephesians 5:19.

Purpose. Music in the Church is not for the entertainment of the people, but rather is an expression of devotion to God. It is natural when men worship together to sing and make melody to the Lord. The best music, when offered to God, promotes noble thoughts and deeds, stimulates faith, fortifies courage, and nourishes the spiritual life. When choirs and congregations sing to the Lord, when musicians play their instruments to the glory of God, there is a far different spirit than that of mere entertainment.

The Rector. Since worship is the primary aim of Church music, it is right that the rector should, according to Canon 24, have the responsibility to employ persons skilled in music, to give orders concerning the music in his parish, and to suppress all that is unseemly and irreverent. Usually the parish priest works in close harmony with the choir director, so that hymns, canticles, and anthems may add to the unity of the service and the beauty of liturgical worship. If services are planned in advance and sermon themes chosen, hymns and anthems carefully selected will speak the same language.

The Choirmaster. The ministry of music in the Church requires professional skill, high standards of character, and a sense of Christian vocation. The true choirmaster is much more than a person paid to run the choir. He is a minister of music, using his talents to uplift the minds and hearts of men in worship. If his office is highly regarded, he will by word and example teach the choir to sing, not for self or for the congregation, but for the glory of God. The singers, by his influence, will strive to be worthy of their high calling as leaders of worship. Petty jealousy, unkind criticism, slovenly work cannot exist when both the clergy and the choirmaster by their attitude teach reverence, loyalty, and devotion to duty.

Volunteer Choirs. It is difficult, when the singers give their services without pay, to obtain regular attendance at rehearsals and services. Many an anthem has been spoiled because some leading voice was absent. Volunteers, however, can be encouraged to be loyal and regular. Some choirs are well organized with officers, such as a secretary to keep records, a music librarian, and even a treasurer. Awards are presented for faithful and regular service. In St. James Church, Atlantic City, N. J., the ribbons and crosses worn signify the length of service. A cross with a white ribbon indicates six months to a year. In the second year the ribbon is red; in the third, yellow; in the fourth, light blue. From the fifth year on, a silver cross is worn with different ribbons for each year. After twenty years service an engraved silver cross is given. This parish also has a choir school taught by the choir director and his assistants, with a four year course, which includes fundamentals of music, history of music, Gregorian music, and hymnody. Examinations are given yearly and choir hoods are awarded in various colors for those who attain 90% or better. In another parish the vestry gives an annual dinner for the choir, at which expressions of appreciation are made and gifts presented. This choir, incidentally, makes its own rules, so that those who miss rehearsals sit in the congregation on Sunday.

Boys' Choirs. It takes a skilled choirmaster who understands boys to conduct and train a good boy choir. To obtain the best results many of our large city parishes have endowed choir schools, where boys can be educated and trained all through the week. Truly glorious music results from this plan at St. Peter's, Philadelphia, and at the Cathedral of St. John the Divine in New York. It is good to have boys in the choir, even in an average parish. Their voices seem especially suited to liturgical music. Many a Christian leader has been deeply influenced by his experiences in a boys' Choir. Usually boys receive some pay for their services, are fined for failures in attendance and conduct, and are given an annual outing or sent to camp.

Junior Choirs. Whenever possible it is good to have a vested choir of children and young people in addition to the regular choir. The junior choir may sing at the services of the Church School, at Lenten services and on special occasions. In some instances, such as at All Saints, Norristown, Pa., the very large number of young people in the junior choir has a real influence on the interest and attendance of parents.

The Congregation. People will sing in church if the conditions are favorable. They will not sing if the hymns are unfamiliar, the canticles difficult, and the choir dominant. Most congregations cannot sing more than 150 hymns. Each parish should have a list of carefully selected hymns. No new hymns will be introduced without preparation. People will learn a new hymn if attention is called, the tune played over, the first verse sung by the choir, and the hymn repeated on several Sundays. New hymns may also be sung as anthems by the choir, with a soloist taking one or more verses. At each service at least one old familiar hymn will be chosen to encourage congrega-

tional singing. Hymnals with music will be placed in
the pews. The people will be asked to rise with the
choir at the first note of the organ. Occasionally the
service can be preceded by a brief period of hymn singing. One parish does this once each month with excellent results in congregational singing.

Processionals. Too frequently the congregation is
excluded from the first and last verses of processionals,
since these are performed as choir pieces with a far
and near effect as the singers enter and disappear. This
effect is changed and the usual bad timing ended, when
the singing begins only after the choir is wholly in the
church. The organ may be played to lead and support
the congregation, not just to accompany the choir. It
is good for singers in procession to keep in step, rather
than to seem like two lines doing a modified snake
dance. The danger, however, is that of swaying from
side to side. Choirs can be taught to march in step
with precision and dignity without the sway.

Canticles, Anthems. Much in music is a matter of
taste. Some delight in Gregorian plainsong; others
much prefer Anglican chants and anthems. A few parishes cling to the "gabble and halt" system of chant-
ing. If congregational singing is desired for the canticles of Morning Prayer, then familiar chants must be
used again and again. People will also learn musical
settings for the Eucharist, if they are really encouraged

to do so. Long, elaborate *Te Deums* ought to be reserved for special occasions. Offertory anthems in the words of Scripture or hymns give ample scope for choirs and soloists to display their skill. Much to be commended is a collection of *Anthems of the Day,* by Morton C. Stone and Ray F. Brown, published in 1952, with Bible passages selected for the Sundays and Holy Days.

Choir Fellowship. Some parishes do not accept the notion that the choir is where temperaments clash, but rather use the ministry of music to promote Christian friendliness. In the great parish of All Saints', Beverly Hills, Calif., where nearly two hundred men, women, and children are in different choirs, nearly seventy-five adult singers meet for a $1.00 supper before the mid-week rehearsal with a definite emphasis on fellowship and concern for each other.

Choir Visits. There is a tendency for choirs to become parochial in outlook and unaware of what goes on in neighboring parishes. This may be changed by choir visits. For example, the girls' choir of a suburban parish came recently to rehearse with the girls of Grace Church, Mt. Airy, Philadelphia, receiving the same careful drill and practice as is usual under the choirmaster, Newell Robinson. For a number of years it was an annual custom for the choirs of Trinity Church, Swarthmore, and Christ Church, Media, Pa., to exchange on the Sunday after Easter Day. This gave the choirs the opportunity to repeat their Easter music to a different congregation and ensured also a large attendance.

✦ 16 ✦

Man Power in the Church

All men to be saved, and to come unto the knowledge of the truth.

—I Timothy 2:4.

Survey. Parishes and communities differ so greatly that often methods that are helpful in one place may not work at all in another. Before making definite plans, a new rector always will survey the situation and gather the facts. One man was told by his predecessor that the men were few in number and indifferent. When, however, a list of names and talents was made, and then a program worked out for and by the men of the parish, the results were astonishing. In this parish, as in many, there was much unused man power.

The Vestry. As a rule the men who serve as vestrymen are truly concerned with the welfare of the Church and willing to work. Some of the clergy hold a narrow view of the sphere of the vestry, limit their activities to financial and material affairs, and vestry meetings may become very dull. Others, on the contrary, encourage active participation in the spiritual life of the parish. It is possible to have vestry committees for Christian education, parish membership, church music, hospitality, and ushering, without infringing on the prerogatives of the rector. The clergy can delegate real responsibility and thus develop lay leadership, or they can try to do it all themselves and let the men remain inactive. It is possible for the rector to have a brief period of spiritual meditation and instruction at every vestry meeting. He may take a Bible passage for comment or present a moral or spiritual problem for discussion. Vestry Corporate Communions and breakfasts are held in some parishes. In a large suburban parish there is always an annual dinner for vestrymen and their wives held at a hotel or country club.

Men at the Altar.   In many places men are asked to serve the priest at the altar at early and late celebrations and to carry the cross for the choir. It is good for boys and young men to see older men of character and ability taking active part in public worship. One parish makes it a rule to schedule men for these duties on one Sunday each month, while the boys and young men take the other Sunday assignments. If there is a guild of servers and acolytes, it helps much to have several older men directing and supervising this work for the clergy.

Lay Readers. It is an astonishing fact that we now have more lay readers in the Episcopal Church than we have clergy. Without the devoted service of these laymen, many small missions and weak parishes would cease to function. It would be well if every parish had several qualified and instructed lay readers to assist in the Church School services, to read lessons and prayers at Morning Prayer, and to be ready in the emergency of the rector's illness to conduct the service. The lay reader is also authorized by canon to read the Epistle in the service of Holy Communion. In the large parish of St. Paul's, Oakland, Cal., it is the custom for the rector to invite outstanding laymen to read the Bible lessons on Sundays from time to time, and also on Wednesday evenings in Lent. In a number of places the custom of having the Daily Offices of Morning and Evening Prayer has been established with the help of several laymen. This is much to be commended. The office of lay reader may be dignified by having men publicly commissioned and given the bishop's license. It is good to seek out men with some experience in public speaking and to challenge them to serve the Church. Some parishes in England invite distinguished public officials on special occasions to come forward from their pews to read the Bible to the congregation. One parish in a college town holds an annual service at which the president of the college reads one lesson and the principal of the local high school the other passage. In St. James' Church, Prospect Park, Pa., there are fourteen lay readers who assist the rector according to a monthly schedule on Sundays and weekdays. They read the Litany, the Epistle, and the Lessons for Morning and Evening Prayer.

Ushers. There is a middle ground between a cold, indifferent attitude toward visitors in church and the overzealous, too hearty welcome. A congregation can be trained to be friendly and alert to make strangers feel at home. It helps greatly to have a guild or committee of ushers with a definite schedule, so that some are present at all services, not only to receive and present the offering, but to stand at the door with the clergy and to secure names and addresses of newcomers. Men who serve thus may be asked by the rector to make friendly calls on new families. One rector uses his ushers to note the absences of regular members to help him tell people they have been missed.

Group Leaders. Despite its obvious difficulties, many parishes use the group system in which the whole parish is divided into districts with men as leaders or captains. Each officer is expected to have several others to assist him and to form the committee for that area. In some places, as in Trinity Church, Swarthmore, Pa., a complete telephone system is arranged, so that messages may be relayed in a short time to every family. The group system enables information concerning sickness, new families, and pastoral problems to be reported promptly to the parish office. From time to time meetings or even "cottage services" are held in each district. In one large parish twelve districts were formed and each street had one house designated as the local headquarters of the church. Notice was given to leaders of forthcoming Baptisms or marriages to promote local interest and parish fellowship. Often a local person would be asked to serve as an unofficial godparent to take a special interest in the new baptized member. This action was usually welcomed heartily by parents. Distribution of parish literature, birthday cards, anniversary greetings was done through the twelve groups. From time to time district parties were held in the parish house to promote fellowship.

Brotherhood of St. Andrew. This fine organization for men and boys was started in Chicago in 1883, but has become international in scope. Brotherhood Chapters for men and Junior Chapters for boys may be organized with the consent of the rector. The two rules of daily prayer and weekly service lead to active participation in the life of the Church. It means much to a parish priest to have a group of laymen meeting regularly for prayer, for spiritual fellowship, and to receive assignments for personal work.

Men's Clubs.   Parish organizations for men along club lines are difficult to maintain. They rise and fall according to the quality of leadership. Some parishes, such as St. Mary's, Ardmore, Pa., have active men's clubs with an interesting program. As a general rule, however, it seems better to have a parish program for men rather than an organization. Such a program may include several Corporate Communions with breakfast and speakers; a men's dinner in the autumn and a father and son dinner in the winter. Some parishes hold forums for men in Advent and Lent with a panel of speakers and opportunity for questions and discussion. These and similar events may be carried out by committees appointed by the rector. Some parishes find it worthwhile to have one weeknight service in Lent sponsored and conducted by the men of the parish. There will then be a choir of men, laymen to read Evening Prayer, and an appropriate sermon by a guest preacher or an address by some layman. In Old St. Peter's Church, Perth Amboy, N. J., the men form the choir on Mother's Day as a tribute to the mothers, while the women reciprocate on Father's Day in June.

Personnel Work.   Every good parish priest becomes by necessity an expert in setting men to work. Far better is it for him to assign tasks to others than to do it himself. Men who serve God and the Church in some active way share in the life of Christian fellowship. Those who merely attend church know little of the sense of belonging and the satisfaction of taking a real part. Busy rectors may be greatly helped by having an informal committee to deal with personnel work, to find suitable tasks for new members, to keep some record of talents and past experience of men.

Retreats.   Many dioceses now have conference centers or retreat houses which afford opportunities for men to have week end retreats. At the conference center of the diocese of Pennsylvania at Radnor, Pa., retreats for men are held regularly, and also groups of vestrymen meet with the bishop. Some rectors have the vestry or the parish council meet there to plan the year's program. Retreats may also be held in a parish church, with the rector or a guest priest as conductor. Several of the Religious Orders make a specialty of conducting retreats.

+ 17 +

Churchwomen in Action

This woman was full of good works.

—ACTS 9:36.

Faithful Women. Without the active support of faithful women, the Christian Church, humanly speaking, could never have survived. Their acts of service are innumerable; their deeds of devotion today in parishes and missions set inspiring examples to the men. Their organizations, of course, are not ends in themselves, but rather effective means whereby the women of the Church may serve God and humanity through the home parish and the world-wide Christian fellowship.

Altar Guild. Since worship is the chief aim of the Church, the care of the sanctuary comes first. It profits a parish little to have successful bazaars while the altar vessels are not cared for properly, the linen soiled or stained, and the House of God dusty and neglected. Always godly women have counted it a high privilege to care for the things of the altar. Usually there is a directress or chairman, appointed by the rector, who makes the assignments for the various tasks to be done each week. In the Church of the Good Samaritan, Paoli, Pa., the rector has asked, not just a few, but a very large number of the parishioners to take responsibility for the altar. Perhaps it would be well if every communicant, at least once a year, had some share in preparing the House of God for worship. Instruction, of course, is necessary and the untrained may be associated with those who have had experience. The best booklet is *An Altar Guild Manual* by Edith Weir Perry, published by Morehouse-Gorham Co. Full information is given about the altar, vessels, vestments, ornaments, directions and suggestions for the altar guild, with suitable prayers and an Office of Admission. It goes without saying that the rector will instruct and guide the guild and conduct from time to time special devotions for the members.

Daughters of the King. This is a Religious Order, founded in 1885, similar to the Brotherhood of St. Andrew, in that there are the two great rules of Prayer and Service. The objective is the spread of Christ's Kingdom, especially among women, and the strengthening of the devotional life of the Church. The official organ is *The Royal Cross.* There are national and diocesan officers and many local chapters.

Woman's Auxiliary: History. This official organization of the Church for women was organized by

General Convention in 1872 as an auxiliary to the Board of Missions, and in 1920 as The Woman's Auxiliary to the National Council. Its aims at first were primarily missionary, while parochial matters were left to the usual ladies' guild. Times have changed. The Woman's Auxiliary is no longer simply a missionary society for those who want to help the heathen in foreign lands. It is rather the one great instrument, through which all the women of the Church may express their faith in action, through the entire life and full program of the Church, beginning with the local parish.

Program, Fields. The program includes worship, study, service, gifts, and fellowship. The fields of service are home, parish, community, diocese, nation, world. This program is carried out by individual prayer and corporate worship; by study of the needs and opportunities in all fields of service; by personal service and generous giving; and by the promotion of real Christian fellowship.

Departments. Both in parishes and dioceses the Auxiliary works through such departments as missions, Christian education, Christian social relations, promotion, finance. Under missions are included foreign, domestic, and diocesan. Christian education aims to increase knowledge of the Church and understanding of her mission through study groups, reading, addresses at meetings. Christian social relations deals with world order and relief, race relations, family life, community welfare. Promotion includes personnel work, enlistment of speakers, publicity. Gifts are made, not only of money through the finance department, but of useful articles, such as clothing, bandages, Church furnishings, etc., through the supply committee.

United Thank Offering.   Every three years at General Convention the women of the Church through the Woman's Auxiliary present to the Presiding Bishop a great sum, recently more than three million dollars, as their thank offering. This is gathered in parishes and missions through the little blue boxes, used to receive gifts to express thankfulness for blessing received. Usually in each local church one woman serves as United Thank Offering chairman. She enlists others to give out and collect the boxes, and plans with the rector for the presentation of this offering.

One Organization.   Experience has proved it better to have one federated organization for all the women in a parish, rather than several competing societies or guilds. If there is one organization for all, then each woman serves and gives in all fields and learns about the whole program of the Church. The Woman's Auxiliary in a parish may include as departments the altar guild, Girls Friendly Society, Daughters of the King, and the Church Periodical Club. Their leaders may be vice presidents, report at the general meetings, and have a share in the budget. The president will not serve more than two years and other offices will be rotated as far as possible. This is easy in a large parish, but difficult when there are few leaders to take responsibility. It is vital to have a common budget for all groups and a general meeting at which reports can be made and action determined.

Chapters, Circles.   The only way all women of the parish can be effectively included is by forming chapters or circles, as intimate friendly groups for congenial persons of similar circumstances. These may be decided by districts or areas, or by common interests, such as young married women, business and professional women, older women, etc. When a parish is quite homogeneous, groups may be formed alphabetically or by districts. When there are wide differences, it is better to let persons join the kind of group that best meets their needs and interests. Large chapters may be divided. All groups will belong to the Woman's Auxiliary, make reports and share in the whole program. Leaders are developed through the chapter plan, since in small meetings in homes or parish house each one is asked to serve in some capacity, to preside as chairman, to lead devotions, to give study reports or to be chapter U.T.O. representative.   In one chapter of fourteen women each one had a definite assignment.

Planning.   The program for meetings and various

affairs throughout the year will be formed well in advance by the officers in consultation with the rector. It helps greatly to have dates for meetings, dinners, bazaars, etc., set far in advance and committees appointed. One parish rotates all assignments that involve much responsibility and work, so that no one person or chapter is responsible for major affairs, such as a parish dinner, more often than once in five years. Many persons and groups are very willing to serve when they know that others will take their proper turn. It is a mistake to overwork the willing and faithful ones.

The Church Periodical Club.   This is one of the cooperating agencies of the National Council which is carried on by the women of the Church. It provides Bibles, Prayer Books, hymnals, and all sorts of books and magazines for people who otherwise could not have them. It started in 1888 when a group of women began sending their Church papers to clergymen who could not afford to subscribe. Today parish branches arrange for Church literature to go to all sorts of needy persons and institutions.

The Rector.   He should be available for consultation with all officers of women's organizations. He will help plan meetings, secure speakers, suggest leaders, but will not be expected to attend always. He may use meetings to talk briefly about important matters. The rector's wife will not hold office, as a rule, but will share actively and assist as much as possible. The rector is the best person to enlist newcomers, to find congenial work for different persons, and to make sure that each woman has an opportunity to serve God and the Church in some useful and suitable way.

Retreats, Days of Intercession. Many rectors find it spiritually profitable to have retreats or quiet days conducted by competent spiritual leaders for the women of the parish. Days of intercession, which begin with an early celebration of the Holy Eucharist and end with Evening Prayer, do much to deepen the spiritual life. Not only the women, but many men as well, are willing to take a set period, fifteen minutes or a half hour, to pray and meditate in the church according to the form suggested by the rector.

✛ 18 ✛

Youth and Age

I have been young, and now am old.

—PSALM 37:25.

Survey.   It is a wise plan for each local Church from time to time to make a survey of the age groups in the parish, to note any shifts or changes, and to consider whether or not the needs of various groups are being adequately met. A community with many young married couples and children requires a different program from a parish where the majority are older people. Often it helps a new rector just to put down the estimated numbers in each age group, and then to look at the parish organizations.

Boys in the Church.   There are various ways in which boys can be organized for Christian service in addition to the Church School and the boys' choir. Quite a few clergy can testify to the lasting influence of the rules of prayer and service in Junior Brotherhood of St. Andrew chapters. Others have found that secret societies, such as Phi Sigma, Pi Alpha, and the Order

of Sir Galahad, with their impressive rites and cere-
monies, have proved effective. Some parishes sponsor
Boy Scout troops, including Cub Scouts, and give
them a room in the parish house. No direct Church
teaching is permitted, but the Scout oath and laws
build sound character. Much can be done if the scout-
master and the troop committee are faithful Church-
men and show it by their example.

Servers, Acolytes. Even the smallest church can
use boys to assist at the altar, to serve as crucifers, and
to carry banners and flags in processions. Some parishes
begin this in the Kindergarten. Active boys need things
to do in church and their interest grows by action. The
wise rector seeks to multiply ways of using boys and
young men in worship. The Order of St. Vincent for
acolytes is a national guild which provides rules, standards, and extra-parochial fellowship. If numbers permit, servers may be divided into older and younger
groups, with monthly meetings, probation for newcomers, admission services, devotional times. Assignments
will be posted, postcards sent as reminders, faithful
work recognized. Some parish priests use a committee
of laymen for instruction. One parish in New York requires an examination in the Prayer Book and Church
symbolism to be passed before full admission. Many
vocations to holy orders have come through service at
the altar in youth. One rector has suppers followed by

meditations for his boys and also takes them on trips to cathedrals and seminaries.

Girls in the Church. Junior Choirs, which sing at Church School services or the Family Service at 9:30 a.m., afford an opportunity for girls to serve in the Church. Junior altar guilds ought to be more common. Many a young girl has been delighted to assist an older woman in flower arrangement on Saturday afternoon in the church. Some parishes use little girls to care for the Church School altars. The Girls Friendly Society, since its founding in England in 1875, has been the largest Episcopal society for girls. Junior members are from seven to fourteen years old; others are from fourteen to twenty-one. The G.F.S. motto is "Bear ye one another's burdens." The program includes worship, study, recreation, and creative activities. Girl Scouts and Camp Fire Girls are similar to the Boy Scouts and are effective in parish life if there is proper leadership.

Young People's Fellowships. Many parishes have youth groups which meet on Sunday evenings. With tactful leadership from the clergy and other adults, the Fellowship may interest and develop young people through programs of worship, instruction, recreation, and service. Without wise leaders the group may degenerate and become a headache for the rector. If possible, there will be a committee of men and women who will sponsor and assist the young people. Perhaps a capable person may be found to serve as unpaid director of young people's work. To put first things first, every meeting will have a brief service of worship conducted by the young people. In one parish the young people had been chiefly concerned with playing games and impatient with worship or instruction. A ten minute service in the church before all events changed this attitude, so that eventually they became proud of their youth services, and invited neighboring groups. Exchange visits to other parishes are helpful. Pilgrimages to Church institutions arouse interest. Every year the Philadelphia Divinity School has a great gathering of youth groups on a Sunday evening for worship and fellowship. One parish holds a monthly communion breakfast for young people. Teams of mothers take turns. Money collected at the table covers all expenses. Some parishes include youth groups in the annual canvass, using their members to visit all young people. The motto of Chi Rho, the high school fellowship group of All Saints, Beverly Hills, Cal., is: "Pray with Christ, Work for Christ, Play for Christ, Learn from Christ." The Young People's Fellowship of Christ Church, 6th and Venango Sts., in Philadelphia, has an average attendance of 97 on Sunday evenings. Evening Prayer is conducted by the young people. There is a short business meeting, followed by a speaker, movie, debate, or panel discussion. This Y.P.F. started a Friday eve-

ning dance, using a rented juke box. The attendance
has averaged 150, enabling the purchase of a record
player and loud speaker. The parish hall has been re-
decorated by the young people, with modern lighting
installed and floors sanded, all by volunteer help. This
Y.P.F. in an industrial area has a well-rounded program of worship, study, service, fellowship, and recreation. Emphasis is laid upon the responsibility of the
young people for the operation of their extensive program. There is a Sports Committee sponsoring basket-
ball, handball, softball, and baseball teams, with records kept and awards given. A Publication Committee
publishes a *Fellowship News* twice each month.

Twenty-Thirty Group.   Many parishes, especially
in larger centers of population, have discovered the
needs of those from twenty to thirty-five years of age.
Holy Trinity Church in Philadelphia has a remarkable
program for scores of young men and women who are
students or hold business or professional positions.
"Supper at Six" for this Trinity Club presented a series on the Arts on first Sundays, vocational Christianity on second Sundays, Religions of the World on
third Sundays, and Personal and Social Problems on
fourth Sundays, with special features on fifth Sundays. Some parishes have strong organizations of young
adults who meet on week nights and reach out for un-
attached and lonely people who may be members of

no religious body. Young married couples also have special interests, which may be met by a club or guild.

Older People.   Recently there has been a rising tide of pastoral interest in older people in the Church. Their increasing numbers have made religious leaders aware of their special needs. Today they constitute nearly 15% of the population, as compared with 7% in 1900 and 3% in 1800. Many rectors have been amazed to learn how many of their parishioners are over sixty-five years old. Because of compulsory retirement, many workers face loss of income and sudden leisure. Illness and loneliness are real problems for the aged. Older people in a parish need to be recognized, appreciated, and given something useful to do.

Church Work for Older People.   Pastoral calling often reveals talents and interests which can be used for the church. A retired banker assists with parish and diocesan finance; an older mechanic does repairs in the parish house; retired business women help with the parish office work. Many older people are willing to serve as delegates to convocations and various diocesan affairs. Some will serve as observers or assistants in the Church School classes. Others will gladly make calls on shut-ins and sick people.

Organized Groups.   Although older people are to be encouraged to join and take a regular part in parish organizations, yet in some places special groups

have been found worthwhile. One parish has a lively
Senior Couples' Club with supper meetings and dances.
Another church sponsors a Golden Age Club for those
sixty-five or older. Some find it effective to have special
events during the year which appeal to older people.
Parish anniversaries, for example, may be used to give
recognition to all who have been members of the parish for twenty-five years or more, with special honor to
the oldest members. Every June in one parish there is
an annual service for married couples, with recognition and gifts for the older couples. One parish uses
Golden Weddings as opportunities for parish celebrations, emphasizing the significance of older people in
the church.

Preaching.   In the preparation of sermons the needs
of the congregation are to be kept in mind. If many
young people are present, each sermon should have
something that reaches them, perhaps an explanation
in plain language or a story illustration. If many older
people are in the congregation, their needs and temptations must not be overlooked by the preacher. One
pastor asked a number of older people to write state-
ments on "What the Church Has Meant to Me" and
then used these in a sermon. Preaching emphasis is
needed on the dignity and worth of human personality,
on values that endure despite physical weakness, on
ways to face life's losses and disappointments.

+ 19 +

Church Publicity

*Let your light so shine before men, that they may
see your good works.*

—St. Matthew 5:16.

Good news. The message of the Christian Church
is good tidings to be made known to all people. In a
broad sense whatever calls the attention to the Church
is religious advertising or publicity. Hence religious
publicity, widely considered, includes the location and
appearance of church buildings, the clerical collar, parish activities, as well as newspaper articles and advertisements, radio broadcasts, and television. If the
Church is to obey the Lord's command to let the light
shine before men, it is evident that all sorts of means
must be employed to that end under modern conditions. In recent years many conservative religious bodies have been making increasing use of various forms
of publicity.

Buildings. Each church building carries a message to all that pass by. The little white church in the

country with a spire pointing up to heaven; the great cathedral rising above the roofs of an ancient city; the stone tower of the city church signifying strength and security; these all speak in their own language. If, however, the country church is unpainted and the grounds poorly kept; if the sidewalks, the fences, the bulletin boards of the city church appear neglected; then the message is not one of hope and welcome. Fortunate is the church which is set upon a hill or stands at a busy intersection or the head of an avenue. Happy is that parish where the people realize the importance of keeping the buildings and grounds clean and beautiful. Some parishes even have garden clubs or paint-and-clean committees, that give time and labor to keep the church property in the best condition.

Outdoor Signs. Many strangers have looked in vain for a sign to say what Church it is and what are the hours of worship. The National Council of the Episcopal Church now has official signs, which can be placed on street corners, to give directions and to express welcome. Outdoor bulletin boards vary from the formal announcement of service hours to the ever-changing, thought-provoking sermon topic. The clergy differ greatly over the question of sermon topics, some never giving in advance their sermon subjects, while others make the titles so striking as to arouse curiosity. One effective use of the outdoor bulletin board consists in posting brief quotations, which may in one sentence or phrase carry a real message. Men have been known to have their lives changed at a critical moment by reading such a display poster. If there is such an outdoor sign, it is important to have some person or committee charged with the duty of keeping it up to date. To read of last Sunday's services on the following Wednesday is bad publicity, and it can be very annoying to a traveler to turn up for a 9 o'clock service when the hour has been changed to 8 o'clock without correcting the notice board.

Indoor Bulletins. Lengthy announcements during services of worship are disturbing to many people. One rector avoids this by skilful use of bulletin boards in the vestibules of the church and parish house. Important matters are featured with striking headlines. Pictures and clippings arouse interest and have teaching value. Lists of names can be posted and appreciation expressed for service rendered.

Parish Papers. Another way to avoid the interruption of worship by announcements is to have a mimeographed or printed parish paper. These vary from costly printed bulletins for large city parishes to the small sheet mimeographed and given out by the ushers. Some pastors find the partly printed, four page weekly paper most useful. These can be obtained from the Department of Promotion of the National Council,

Morehouse-Gorham Co., or the Diocese of Chicago. Best of all, in the opinion of many, is the weekly parish paper, which is entered as second class matter and mailed to reach every family just before Sunday. This weekly can tell of the Sunday services and the events of the coming week, as well as the record of past activities in the church. Such a paper serves as a parish visitor, for it knocks at the door of each home, and reminds people of the call to worship and the work and fellowship of the church. The monthly paper, of course, is excellent for news of past events and affords space for articles about religion and the church. Both weekly and monthly papers can be maintained at little or no expense to the parish treasury, provided that business ads are used and subscriptions received. The rector may serve as editor, but it is best to have an experienced layman as business manager. In one New Jersey parish, the parish paper is edited, produced, and maintained by committees of parishioners who take a keen interest in this task.

Yearbooks. Many of the large parishes produce yearbooks which give complete reports of the activities of the previous year. In Philadelphia, for example, Christ and St. Michael's Church in Germantown and St. Stephen's Church on Tenth St. have notable year books with interesting articles and many pictures.

Newspapers. Publicity is of little value unless there is something worthwhile to make known. If the parish program is full of interest, the general public will want to read about it in the daily press. Every clergyman can learn the proper methods of writing acceptable news articles. The busy rector will also get the help of men and women who are experienced in journalism. One pastor has a publicity committee composed of experts who give their services in various ways. The gist of a news story must be given in the opening sentence, with details coming later. Clean, typewritten copy, with wide margins and spaces, is expected. One will keep in mind for a good news story the six words or questions: What? When? Where? Who? Why? and How? Short sentences and plain language are expected. Many newspapers will print extracts or interesting paragraphs from Sunday sermons, provided that they are received on the previous Friday. Visiting preachers in the Cathedral of St. John the Divine, New York, are often asked to send in such sermon extracts in advance, so that they may appear in Monday's papers. Rarely, however, should the full sermon be sent to a newspaper; the editor will probably not have the time to read it or the space to publish it.

Church Advertisements.   It is customary for newspapers to print on Saturday the Church page with religious news and paid ads. Opinions differ concerning the value of large paid notices of religious services. However, there seems to be an increasing use of them in many cities. Some stress sensational sermon topics, while others give a brief message or a sermonette. The Knights of Columbus have used paid ads to arouse interest and invite inquiry, with good results. In our own Church, the Diocese of Iowa has also used paid ads successfully. Their "copy" may be obtained on request. If your parish is in a summer or winter resort area, or in a location where there are frequent visitors, it will be most helpful to those visitors if the hours of service or any special services are advertised in the local newspaper during the appropriate season.

Radio and Television. In many cities and communities it is not unusual to have entire services of worship broadcast by local radio stations. Carol services or other musical events are especially suitable for broadcast. Ministers need to make the best use of radio publicity and to learn how to speak easily and naturally before the microphone. In recent years all sorts of services have been televised, including the consecration of a bishop and the celebration of a Christmas or Easter Eucharist.

Printing, Mail. Church publicity includes good use of printed material, from the rector's calling cards to the printed letters sent out to all parishioners. One pastor has a small sketch of the church tower printed on the corner of his calling card. Another has the hours of worship and an invitation on his card. Still another carries a larger printed card in color, with a cut of the church, the hours of services, and a cordial invitation. This is left with new families or placed under the door or in the mailbox. Printed or multigraphed letters, signed by hand, and sent first-class often produce real results. Nothing, of course, can equal the value of a personal letter, written by hand.

✛ 20 ✛

The Parish and the Community

In brotherly charity one towards another.

—Book of Common Prayer, p. 48.

Responsibility.   Every parish or mission has a real responsibility for the community in which it is located. In a small town or city the minister is recognized as a leading citizen. He is invited to share in community affairs and expected to make his influence count for righteousness and progress. As a general rule, the members of a congregation are pleased to have their pastor take a prominent part in community life, since he is their representative in all good works. There is always, however, the danger of giving too much time to community organizations to the neglect of the parish. Even in large metropolitan centers, like New York and Chicago, the clergy often exercise real influence in the neighborhoods where they live and work.

Friendly contacts.   It is quite possible for the Christian pastor, even in large cities, to establish many friendly relationships outside his congregation. In one city the new rector introduced himself promptly to the principal of the high school, the police captain of his district, the Y.M.C.A. officers, and the business men near his church. Much favorable comment and good-will resulted. He was invited to give the invocation at a Chamber of Commerce dinner and asked to address the parents and teachers in the high school. Before long he found that he had many friendly contacts and was in a position of real influence in the community. If a man has a definite rule of study and pastoral work, he will be able to share in community affairs without neglecting his main business.

Church members. An active parish exercises a real power in its community through the members. If the Gospel is preached in all its fullness, Christian people will realize their privilege and their duty to act and serve as Christians in politics, government, business, education, and recreation. One of the causes of crime and corruption in our cities is the fact that too many Christians hold aloof from community life. Far better is it for the pastor to inspire men and women to serve as Christians than for him to try to do it all himself. To be specific, capable men and women in the congregation ought to be found serving in such fields as the Community Chest, the Red Cross, Y.M.C.A., Boy Scouts, Girl Scouts, Camp Fire Girls, and Parent-Teacher Associations.

Religions. The Christian minister will take a friendly interest in other religious leaders in his vicinity and in the work being carried on by them. There is much to be gained by friendliness and co-operation. Without sacrificing any principles, one may belong to ministerial associations and share in many co-operative efforts. A friendly call on a new clergyman or a letter of welcome will be much appreciated. The problem of union services varies in different places. As a general rule, it is better to share in union services on special occasions, particularly in smaller communities, than to hold aloof. The Archbishop of Canterbury, for example, co-operated in the Billy Graham evangelistic services in London.

Recreation. Because of the increase in leisure time in every community more hours are being given to amusements, sports, theatres, and country clubs. Here also there is an opportunity for the Christian leader, but a constant danger lest he fall into one of two extremes. He may keep entirely apart from the social and recreational life of the community, losing thereby in understanding and friendly relationships. Or he may go too far in his interest in these things, so that he becomes known as a bridge-playing, golfing, worldly parson. There is here, as always, a middle ground for discretion and common sense. Wholesome recreation is good for the clergy. Many a rector has found his influence enhanced, especially among young men, because he has shown an interest in sports and taken an active part in some games. When possible, the parish house may become a center of recreation, where, under Christian auspices, dances, bridge parties, plays, and athletic contests may take place. Such a program may have a definite effect in reducing juvenile delinquency and in avoiding the temptations and excesses of country club life.

Smoking, Drinking, Gambling.   Because of a reaction from Puritanism, many Church members see no harm in smoking, drinking, and in playing games for money, provided that these are not carried to excess. It is difficult to make rules for other people, for in some matters each must decide for himself. The Christian minister must consider, not himself, but his office and work. There may be no harm in smoking, but if he goes to the altar to celebrate the Holy Communion or to the hospital to visit one critically ill, with his breath and his clothes reeking with tobacco, the result is not good. There may be no harm in drinking a cocktail with friends in a home, but if one's example does lead others to excess, it is better to abstain. Unfortunately, more than one man in holy orders has surprised himself and others by becoming an alcoholic. Betting on horses is legal in some states, and so also is bingo and various games of chance. It is a good rule for the clergy to take no part in these and to make sure that no gambling affairs take place in the parish house.

Hospitals, Courts, Prisons.   Every parish priest will reckon visiting the sick a primary duty. This means that he will become a familiar figure in the local hospital, visiting not only the members of his church, but being available to minister to those of any or no religion. Many hospital contacts have proved fruitful in leading to new members for the Church. The Christian minister and his people can serve their community through courts and prisons. One clergyman visited the courthouse, became acquainted with the county judge, served on the grand jury, gained much in understanding and influence. Another found that no Sunday services were held in the county jail, so he persuaded others to join in this ministry and rendered valuable service. Many legal authorities believe that the standards of courts would be improved if Christian people in general would accept jury duty as a service to the community and not avoid such a responsibility.

Parish Action.   It is a good rule that the Church as an organized body should stay out of politics. It is best for the action to come through individual members who act in political parties and in the civic life of the community. There are times, however, when the parish has a corporate responsibility to arouse the conscience of the community to political evils, social dangers, or manifest needs. There are times when the church must care for the friendless and the neglected. These situations may call for such positive action as the Church has taken in the past. Many parishes have taken the lead in establishing schools, hospitals, and day nurseries. It is the duty of the Church to give its members ideals of service, that they may have something worthwhile to accomplish. Too many modern people are busy with petty and selfish concerns. When the citizens of a community live in the true faith and fear of God, they will exercise brotherly charity one towards another. By friendly words and kindly deeds community spirit grows, until men begin to take pride in their town and to think of it as a colony of heaven.

✦ 21 ✦

The Diocese and
the General Church

*Ye shall be witnesses unto me both in Jerusalem,
and in all Judea, and in Samaria, and unto the
uttermost part of the earth.*

—Acts 1:8.

Parochialism. When a local Church thinks too much about its own affairs and too little about the whole cause of Christ's Church, it is rightly called parochial. No parish exists for itself and none is complete by itself. Just as persons are baptized to be members of the whole Body of Christ; just as the clergy are ordained to be priests of the Holy Catholic Church, so the parishes are local groups whose real significance comes from their membership in the diocese and the general Church. When a local congregation becomes able to pay its own expenses, it ceases to be a mission and becomes a parish. Both missions and parishes, however, are expected to belong to the larger fellowship, and have the duty and privilege of sharing in the

164

support of the program of the diocese and the Church in the nation and abroad.

Diocese. When a missionary district has increased in numbers and strength so that it can maintain itself, it becomes a diocese, having a bishop chosen by its own clergy and laity in convention. Such election, however, must be approved by bishops and standing committees of other dioceses, showing that the diocese stands not alone by itself, but shares in the larger life of the Church. The diocese, however, much more than the parish, is a complete unit of the Church, having the three orders of the ministry, bishop, priests and deacons, as well as the laity. The Episcopal Church in the United States in 1955 had seventy-five dioceses. Each diocese, as a rule, holds an annual convention with the bishop as presiding officer, all the clergy as clerical delegates, three lay persons from each parish and one from each mission. When there is no diocesan bishop, the standing committee, elected by the convention, becomes the ecclesiastical authority.

Missionary Districts. A territory or group of local congregations, unable to maintain themselves and to pay the salary of a bishop, is called a missionary district. The bishop for this district is elected by the House of Bishops and an appropriation is made from the treasury of the National Council of the Church. The annual meeting of the bishop, the clergy, and the lay representatives of a missionary district is usually called a convocation. There are twelve domestic missionary districts, five extra-continental, and ten overseas or foreign missionary districts aided or supported by the Episcopal Church in the United States.

Bishops. According to the Book of Common Prayer, there have been in Christ's Church from the time of the apostles three orders of ministers: bishops, priests, and deacons. A diocesan bishop today is one charged with the responsibility and oversight of a diocese. His duties are manifold: visitation of churches and administering Confirmation; supervision of men preparing for the ministry and Ordination; administration of the canons and laws of the Church; direction of the missionary work in the diocese. He is expected to be the spiritual leader of the whole diocese and the father in God to his clergy, but too often he is overburdened with administrative work. A missionary bishop has the same responsibilities in a missionary district. A coadjutor bishop is elected to assist the diocesan, but has definite duties assigned to him, and possesses the right of succession. A suffragan bishop assists the diocesan as he is requested, and has no right to succeed the diocesan. In the Anglican Communion, except in the United States, bishops may be translated from one diocese to another. In the American Church only missionary and suffragan bishops may be called to another diocese.

Provinces.   A group of dioceses and missionary districts form a province, as for example, the first province comprises the seven dioceses of New England. In the United States one of the bishops of a province is elected as president, whereas in the Anglican Communion generally the head of a province is known as an archbishop. There are eight provinces in the United States; four in Canada; two (Canterbury and York) in England; one in Wales; two in Ireland; one in Scotland. When the bishops and clerical and lay deputies of a province meet it is called a synod. Although this body has litle power to legislate, there are many who feel that it would be good for the Church if more responsibility were laid upon the provinces. For example, it would be a forward step if each province were to have standard examinations for candidates for holy orders, instead of leaving this entirely to each diocese.

General Convention.   The governing body of the American Episcopal Church is known as General Convention. Every three years four clerical and four lay deputies are sent from each diocese. Each missionary district is entitled to one clerical and one lay deputy. The House of Bishops includes all bishops, diocesan, retired, coadjutor, suffragan, missionary. The House of Deputies functions in two orders, clerical and lay. Both houses must concur for legislation.

Presiding Bishop.   Although at first the office of Presiding Bishop was filled by seniority, at present one of the bishops is elected by General Convention. He must resign his jurisdiction and is chosen for the remainder of his active episcopate. His official seat is in Washington Cathedral; his business office at Church Missions House, New York City; his residence at Dover House in Greenwich, Conn. The Presiding Bishop is the executive head of the Protestant Episcopal Church in the United States of America.

National Council. This body, whose President is the Presiding Bishop, *ex officio,* is composed of twenty persons (bishops, priests and lay persons), elected by General Convention, and one from each of the eight provinces. The whole program of the Church is directed through the National Council by means of six departments. These are: Overseas (Foreign Missions); Home (Domestic Missions, College work, Armed Forces, Rural); Christian Education (Children, Curriculum, Adult, Leadership Training, Youth, Audio-Visual, Seabury Press); Christian Social Relations (Health and Welfare, Christian Citizenship, Urban-Industrial); Promotion (Publications, Public Relations, Radio and Television); Finance.

Lambeth Conference. In the Anglican Communion each national Church is independent, with no control by any foreign bishop or legislative body. The Archbishop of Canterbury, by general consent, is given the primacy of honor. Beginning in 1867, by his invitation, bishops of the Anglican Church throughout the world have met at Lambeth Palace in London about every ten years to consider problems before the Church and to pass resolutions. These actions have no legislative power, but exercise great influence.

Assessments, Quotas. Each local church is usually given an assessment to be paid for the support of the episcopate and the diocese. This must be paid or the church loses its lay vote in convention. Each parish and mission is also assigned a quota for the support of the whole program of the Church. This quota is based, not upon membership, but upon the amounts spent by the congregation upon such current expenses as salaries, music, heat, and light. This quota is an obligation of honor, not to be lightly disregarded because of selfish parochialism, but to be so strongly presented that all will count it a privilege and a duty to share in the vast program of the Church. Missionary sermons are to be preached by rectors and by visiting clergy. Throughout the year, and not just at canvass time, the people are to be informed concerning various aspects of the Church's general program. Parish delegates ought to be encouraged to go to diocesan meetings. Each parish organization is to be guided to include in its program some missionary projects. The Church School and Lenten study classes can be vital factors in giving information and arousing enthusiasm for the advance work of the Church at home and abroad.

Publications. In parishes where people are informed, there is little difficulty in raising quotas. It would help much if such Church publications as *Forth, The Living Church,* and *Episcopal Churchnews,* were read in the homes of our people. One rector makes sure that every vestryman subscribes to *Forth* and to the diocesan magazine. Another parish makes an annual campaign to secure subscriptions to Church publications. Another has a bulletin board in the parish house on which clippings are placed from religious papers. It has been proved over and over that interest in the worldwide work of the Church never decreases giving to local needs, but on the contrary, the more people know about the general Church and give generously to this cause, the more the local parish will flourish.

✦ 22 ✦

Business Methods in the Church

Let all things be done decently and in order.

—I Corinthians 14:40.

Ideals. A few persons may have the notion that business methods do not belong in the Church, since a man of God need not concern himself with such mundane matters as records, files, and reports. St. Paul, just before he wrote the great resurrection chapter in First Corinthians, warned his converts against the dangers of confusion and the importance of doing all things decently and in order. If God Himself is the God of order, then the most orderly way of doing things is God's way. Every dedicated minister will be a spiritual craftsman, striving to use the best methods in his study and office, as well as out among his people.

Common Sense. We all know, however, that there is a danger of too much emphasis upon details, red tape, and statistics. Church work is essentially spiritual. Quantitative standards do not always apply. Pastoral success cannot be measured by mere numbers in a report. Good judgment is needed lest the determination to be businesslike lead religious workers away from the primary concerns of the Church.

Parish Records. First in importance is the register of such official ministerial acts as baptisms, confirmations, marriages, burials, together with the record of communicants and transfers. This is the responsibility of the rector or vicar. Items ought to be entered promptly. Delay is dangerous. No one has the right to be careless or haphazard with records that concern the lives of people and their legal rights. A cross index is helpful when certificates are requested. This may be alphabetical or each may be given a key number, by which his entire history in the register may be traced.

History. The rector and the wardens will take care for the historical documents of the parish, such as the charter or certificate of incorporation, the consecration record, the minute books of the vestry. It would be worthwhile for a history of the parish to be kept up-to-date, with a list of the clergy with dates, a list of wardens and vestrymen, and other records and facts. Perhaps a historiographer might be appointed for the parish, who would take pride in keeping such matters properly recorded. All valuable documents ought to be properly listed, with information as to where they are kept.

Office Files. Metal files with locks are best for the

confidential records of Church membership and finances. Access to these is limited to the pastor, the secretary, and other authorized persons. There will be a
card index of families and individuals, alphabetically,
with addresses and other information. This must be
kept up-to-date with changes promptly recorded. In
large parishes, where paid secretaries are employed,
there will be geographical records of members in districts; organization lists, a correspondence file, and a
section for official documents.

Financial Records.   The treasurer or financial secretary will keep a record of the gifts, pledges and pay-
ments of all members, also an account of all receipts
and disbursements. These are confidential matters to
be kept under lock in the office. An annual audit will,
of course, be made.

Rector's Records.   Each minister would do well to
keep a history of his own ministry and a record of all
his official acts. In later years he will appreciate the
value of this, when he can no longer consult the reg-
isters of parishes he has served. If he lives at a distance
from the parish office, he will need a duplicate list of
church members and addresses. He needs also a loose-
leaf book for parish calling, arranged by streets and
districts. An anniversary file, one card for each day of
the year, will enable him to recall birthdays and other
anniversaries. It is helpful also to have lists of new

families, unbaptized and unconfirmed persons, sick and shut-in people.

Reports. An annual report to the bishop is required and too often these are unduly delayed for lack of available information. If a proper record is kept at the church of each service held (suitable books are provided for this), if the membership statistics are up to date in the card index and the parish register, then the financial report can be added and the report completed. Some rectors make a monthly report of their official acts and keep a record day by day of baptisms, marriages, burials, calls, and meetings. This requires a man to be systematic, orderly, and active. In some parishes monthly or quarterly reports are made of finances and of all parish organizations.

Personal Files. In addition to official acts, each minister will keep a record of his sermons and addresses in a sermon record book, with texts, dates, and places. Sermons on cards may be numbered S1, S2, etc., and kept in metal boxes or drawers. For clippings, notes, magazine articles, etc., the file folders of the standard size are best. These may be arranged in a filing cabinet alphabetically. It is better, however, to use the Dewey system of classification which is used in all public libraries. For a small amount the Abridged Decimal Classification book can be secured with numbers and index for all subjects and topics. The books, clippings, and notes in the pastor's study can then be systematically arranged and indexed so as to make immediately available whatever is desired. It is possible also to use 3x5 and 4x6 cards on which to type quotations, illustrations, verses, stories, which may be numbered, filed, and used in sermons and addresses.

Correspondence.   Too many of the clergy are careless about answering letters, little realizing how discourteous this is. When an invitation, for example, comes for one to preach or to address a meeting, and there is no reply for days or weeks, a very bad impression is made. If possible, all business letters are to be answered within two days. Replies should be brief with the main thought at the beginning of the letter. Church stationery will be dignified, with the name of the church and the rector's name and address. The letterhead may be improved by having a small engraving of the spire, the tower, or parish seal. Some rectors write many personal letters of appreciation and congratulation. Two or three sentences in the handwriting of a busy pastor mean much to the people. Some use dictaphones and have paid or volunteer secretaries later transcribe these. Form letters to the parish produce results if signed personally.

Engagements.   The busy city pastor who works under much pressure with many services, meetings, and interviews, must live by his engagement book. It is unpardonable to forget a wedding or a funeral. Even in the country parish today the pastor must schedule his time carefully and set aside definite times for study and sermon preparation. One day each week ought to be scheduled in advance for rest or recreation. Certain times and occasions will be for the home and family. Only emergency calls will be allowed to interfere.

Leadership. Church work is mainly carried on by volunteers who give their services because of their devotion and love for Christ and His Church. This makes the parish quite different from a business which pays dividends and wages. It requires tact, management, and leadership to secure all the voluntary co-operation and teamwork that is needed. The business expert can offer promotion and higher wages. The pastor depends on interest and loyalty. He strives to enlist all his people in the worship and work of the Church. He becomes a personnel expert, studying the talents of his members and placing them in tasks interesting and worthwhile. Much pastoral calling can provide opportunities for personnel work. The active parishioner is an asset; the inactive member is in danger of lapsing. Pastoral leadership consists not in the voice of authority, but rather in planning, in making suggestions, in encouraging teamwork, in helping officers and members to understand problems and to advocate progressive ways and means. It is a major error to decide things without consultation, to propose programs without previous discussion. Many failures result from closed lines of communication.

Building Campaigns.   When a special effort is to be made to build a new church or parish house, it ought to be preceded by a survey of the situation and a study of the needs. Expert help can be secured from the diocese, from experienced clergy and laymen, and from professional money-raising firms. Most rectors are convinced that it is far better to secure professional help in building campaigns than to try to accomplish this with volunteers.

✦ 23 ✦

This Ministry

Ye are called . . . to be Messengers, Watchmen, and Stewards of the Lord.

—Book of Common Prayer, p. 539.

Messengers. From the very beginning Christianity has been a Gospel, a message of good tidings for all people. Jesus Himself came as the Word of God Incarnate, revealing God to men, teaching and interpreting divine truth. The very genius of the Church is communication of God to mankind. The Christian preacher has the dignity and privilege of being God's messenger, communicating the thoughts of God to men in language they will understand. Apostles, prophets, evangelists— all are men sent out with a message from God.

Watchmen. The Christian pastor is a watchman, guarding against dangers, warning against evils. Like a sentry he protects the people of God from the assaults of sin, suffering, and death. He is the good shepherd, the pastor who loves people and gladly gives his life in service to them. In pastoral counseling he

178

perceives the temptations and dangers; guards against ignorance, misunderstanding, prejudice; strengthens and comforts the weak; helps all to right decisions.

Stewards.   The parish priest is the steward of God's mysteries, holding, as it were, the keys to the divine storehouse, giving access to the sacramental treasures of grace and power. He administers the sacraments as the representative of the great High Priest, holding a sacred trust, having a strong faith in the power of God released through these holy channels.

Holiness.   The minister of Christ is called to a life of holiness. By his ordination he is set apart, dedicated, stamped indelibly with God's mark. He is to be a man of God, walking on holy ground, handling sacred things, carrying with him the presence of God. As shepherd of souls, dealing with human lives and destinies, he is on holy ground. When he baptizes little children, when he prepares young people for confirmation, when a couple come to be married, when there is sickness and death in the home he visits, the priest and pastor represents the Holy God and must be a man of God. Above all, when he stands at the altar, when he administers the Body and Blood of Christ to the faithful, he is no longer just himself with all his peculiarities, but rather he is God's priest, in the very holy of holies of the sanctuary.

Discipline.   It follows then, that the true priest and

pastor, realizing his own unworthiness for this high privilege, will be a man of discipline. He will have a rule of life, with set times for prayer and meditation. Despite his manifold duties and the pressure of the world upon him, there will be the steady uplift of the Daily Offices, of the practice of the presence of Christ, of habits of reading and study. Most men find the early morning best for the life of devotion. Some have rules of reading so many books each month, not fiction, and a reading record that becomes a judgment against neglect.

Temptations. Because the clergy are human, they are subject to temptations. One may magnify the office, but realize in all humility how unworthy is the best of men to be the ambassador of Christ. When a minister falls into sin, he gives occasion for many to stumble, and brings reproach upon the Church of Christ. Besides the grosser sins, obvious to all, there are special temptations for the clergy. There is sloth or laziness, the temptation to sleep late, to do as little work as possible, to let one's rule of life go by default. In the ministry there is no boss to check one's working hours, to force one to pray, read, study. There is vanity, the pleasure one gets in being honored and flattered as "Reverend" and "Father"; the love of display, reading services as an actor performing before an audience, in an affected, ecclesiastical voice. There is the temptation to think of "my Church," "my parish," "my sermon," instead of saying with St. Paul, "Not I, but Christ liveth in me." There is discouragement or impatience, whereby a man loses hope because God does not hurry things to get results. There is self-indulgence or impurity, which like a canker eats away at the center of life and destroys the power of one's ministry. There is also envy and jealousy of other ministers, who may seem more fortunate, and the temptation to criticize and gossip.

Personal Conduct. In no other vocation or profession does a man's personality count for so much. He must show himself worthy of the respect, the trust, and the affection of his congregation. He is a marked man in the community, so that slovenly dress, soiled linen, careless speech, and habits of self-indulgence will destroy his influence. He must be absolutely honest and sincere in all his dealings, lest unpaid debts and questionable practices ruin his credit. Good manners, courtesy, gentleness, kindliness are expected of him, since he is the accredited representative of One who has been called the most perfect Gentleman of all history, even Jesus Christ.

Recreation, Health. The work of the minister of Christ is never done and there are times when he will be busy in pastoral duties far beyond an eight hour day. It is advisable for him to have one day off each week, perhaps Monday after a heavy Sunday schedule; perhaps Saturday, as a physical and mental preparation for the Lord's Day. A healthy body, kept fit by fresh air and exercise, will enable a man to do his best work. The ability to relax, to flop for a few minutes, perhaps to take a short nap in the midst of a busy day, is a valuable accomplishment.

Fellowship.   Since the Church of Christ is a holy fellowship, there ought to be among all the clergy a deep spirit of friendly co-operation. Too often this fellowship appears to be lacking. Charity, brotherly love, mutual helpfulness ought to prevail instead of competition, criticism, and discourtesy. Leaders of other religious bodies are to be regarded as other pastors and shepherds employed by the One Good Shepherd, rather than as rivals whose sheep are to be stolen if possible.

Opportunity.   The Christian ministry affords the greatest opportunity for service of any vocation. Literally all doors are open to him who comes in the name of the Lord. Wearing the uniform of the man of God, he may go at all times to schools, hospitals, prisons, asylums. His co-operation is welcomed by officials of all sorts. Among his people he touches life from the cradle to the grave, not waiting to be called as the physician and lawyer must do, but going to all homes where there is need, bringing the confidence of a certain faith and the comfort of a reasonable, religious, and holy hope. His work is essential to the welfare of humanity, for where there is no vision, the people perish. In the name of Christ and by the power of the Holy Spirit, he battles with the enemies of mankind, finding his deepest joy and reward in doing the Master's will.

Index